Library of
Davidson College

AMERICAN PHILOSOPHICAL QUARTERLY
MONOGRAPH SERIES

AMERICAN PHILOSOPHICAL QUARTERLY
MONOGRAPH SERIES

Edited by NICHOLAS RESCHER

STUDIES IN MORAL PHILOSOPHY

Essays by:

David Braybrooke
Lawrence Haworth
G. P. Henderson
Jesse Kalin
Kai Nielsen
Jerome B. Schneewind

Michael Stocker

Monograph No. 1   Oxford, 1968

PUBLISHED BY BASIL BLACKWELL
WITH THE COOPERATION OF THE UNIVERSITY OF PITTSBURGH

© *in this collection Basil Blackwell 1968*
631 11450 5

PRINTED IN ENGLAND
by C. Tinling & Co. Ltd., Liverpool, London and Prescot

CONTENTS

Editor's Preface
   NICHOLAS RESCHER 7

On Moral Truth
   KAI NIELSEN 9

On Ethical Egoism
   JESSE KALIN 26

Moral Nihilism
   G. P. HENDERSON 42

Supererogation and Duties
   MICHAEL STOCKER 53

Utility and Rights
   LAWRENCE HAWORTH 64

Let Needs Diminish That Preferences May Prosper
   DAVID BRAYBROOKE 86

Whewell's Ethics
   JEROME B. SCHNEEWIND 108

Index of Names 143

EDITOR'S PREFACE

With this volume, the *American Philosophical Quarterly* inaugurates its supplementary Monograph Series, which will, it is hoped, prove a welcome addition to the limited existing channels for the publication of technical philosophy within the English-language area.

The essays gathered together here are a palpable token of the vitality and many-sidedness of thought on issues of ethics and moral philosophy in the Anglo-American orbit. The *American Philosophical Quarterly* is most grateful to the learned contributors for permitting the inclusion of their essays in this collection.

The editor is indebted to Miss Dorothy Henle for her able assistance in seeing the work through the press.

Nicholas Rescher
Pittsburgh, 1967

I
On Moral Truth
KAI NIELSEN

WHEN we reflect philosophically about morality we are very typically concerned with determining whether we can have any knowledge of good and evil, whether any moral claims have an objective rationale; that is to say, in thinking about the foundations of moral belief, we want very much to know whether any ethical code or any moral claim at all can be shown to be objectively justified.

In making such an inquiry, we run into trouble right away. What does it mean to say that moral claims can be objectively justified? Presumably it means that some moral claims are objective. But what does *that* mean? Some moral philosophers write as if moral judgments or moral statements would be objective if and *only* if moral values had a real existence apart from any reference to a human mind or to human attitudes. But now we are surely up queer street, for moral values are not objects like a table or even like an electron. To speak of moral values is to speak of what is good or right *to do*, or to *have done*, or what is good to seek, or of what one ought to be or to have been. But then we are surely not talking of what exists but of what is *to be* brought into existence. Sometimes we do indeed make assertions about what is the case when we make moral judgments, e.g., when we assert that someone has an admirable character, but moral utterances usually involve a *telling to*, not a *telling that*. (In talking about the past we are talking about what to have done.) Given this peculiarity of moral discourse, it is absurd to think of moral values as some peculiar sort of "non-natural object" or of norms as existing in some odd noumenal realm. If we note the actual uses of moral discourse we will immediately recognize that it is absurd to think of moral values as existing either apart from or as being dependent on human minds. Talk of existence cannot gain a foothold here. Moral values are neither natural nor non-natural objects. To ask whether in that sense they are objective is like asking whether a wife is unmarried. Such a request is self-refuting because it is nonsensical.

Yet, as Westermarck recognized, though he was not entirely free of the above kind of confusions, there are other, quite separable elements in the concept of an objective moral judgment that perhaps can be satisfied. First, if someone is claiming that the statements "x is good" or "x is wrong" are objective statements, he is claiming, at the very least, that such statements are not reducible to x is *thought* to be good or x is *thought* to be wrong. If our moral claims are objective, they must be something of which we could correctly say that though people *think* so and so is wrong, they are mistaken, for it is not wrong. There are people who think that the earth is flat but their thinking so does not make the earth flat. Only if we can get beyond "thinking makes it so" can we be justified in claiming that there are objective moral claims.

Westermarck adds another condition that must be satisfied if moral judgments can be correctly said to be objective. This is the condition that some moral judgments can be true and others false. To believe in the objectivity of morals is to believe that some moral statements are true. In short, to correctly claim that a certain "course of conduct is objectively right, it must be thought to be right by all rational beings who judge truly of the matter and cannot, without error, be judged to be wrong." Now we must be careful here to use the word "rational" in a non-moralistic way, if we are to avoid going in a short and vicious circle.[1] In short, to assert "x is objectively right" and "x is objectively speaking the best thing to do" is to give one to understand that statements asserting that x is objectively right or that x is objectively speaking the best thing to do are true and that they are thought to be true by all rational beings who properly consider the matter. But apart from difficulties about "rational" and "properly consider the matter," there are notorious difficulties about saying moral statements are true or false. I want here to consider these difficulties.

Most emotivists and other non-descriptivists claim that it is misleading to say that fundamental moral statements are either true or false.[2] They readily admit that it is linguistically quite in order to say of certain very typical moral statements that they are true or false. In that way they differ very markedly from commands or imperatives or mere expressions of emotion. A. J. Ayer puts this general point very well when he remarks:

[1] It is used in a moralistic way in the following examples. "A rational man will never simply use people to further his own interests," "A rational man will not pursue his own lesser good at the expense of the greater good of his society," "A rational man will be fair in his dealings with others."

[2] I say *most*, for C. L. Stevenson makes it quite evident that he does not think it is misleading. See C. L. Stevenson, *Facts and Values* (New Haven, 1963), pp. 214–220.

For, as the English language is currently used—and what else, it may be asked, is here in question?—it is by no means improper to refer to ethical utterances as statements; when someone characterizes an action by the use of an ethical predicate, it is quite good usage to say that he is thereby describing it; when someone wishes to assent to an ethical verdict, it is perfectly legitimate for him to say that it is true, or that it is a fact, just as if he wished to dissent from it, it would be perfectly legitimate for him to say that it was false. We should know what he meant and we should not consider that he was using words in an unconventional way.[3]

Ayer stresses all this, but he still argues, as have many others, that it is logically misleading to follow ordinary usage here. These non-descriptivists are recommending a new way of speaking that will be, so they think, logically speaking less misleading than the old way of speech. Ayer argues that when we consider carefully the actual use of moral language—its depth grammar rather than its surface grammar—we will see that moral utterances, even when declarative in form, are not verifiable or even confirmable. If I say "The dog is in the snow," "The Russians are invading Alaska," or "Frustrated people tend to respond with aggression" you know what facts count in establishing the truth or falsity of my claim. These statements assert certain quite empirically identifiable states of affairs which, if the asserted state of affairs in question actually does exist, will establish the truth of my claim. If it does not exist then my claim can quite correctly be said to be false. My attitudes, my interests, do not at all affect the truth or falsity of what I assert. I may hate to see dogs romping in the snow, I may fear the Russians coming to Alaska, I may deplore the fact that frustrated people keep the whole cycle going by responding aggressively, but all the same the facts are what they are no matter how I or anyone else may feel about them. But how do we verify or confirm, falsify, or disconfirm "Dogs ought to be allowed to romp in the snow," "The Russians ought not to invade Alaska," or "Frustrated people ought not to become aggressive"? We can and do give reasons for these statements, but what would it be like to verify the statements as distinct from verifying whether some of the factual statements given as supporting reasons are true? There seem to be no facts that we can point to that would verify such statements; and if there is no *conceivable* direct verification of them then we cannot sensibly speak of an indirect verification of them either, for where nothing could conceivably count as direct verification the phrase "indirect verification" could have no meaning. If this is so, we do not know what it would be like for such claims to be true, for

[3] A. J. Ayer, "On the Analysis of Moral Judgments" in Milton Munitz (ed.), *A Modern Introduction to Ethics* (New York, 1958), p. 537.

we do not know what we would have to apprehend to make them true or, for that matter, false. Because of this, Ayer argues, we had better, for philosophical purposes at least, amend ordinary language and stop speaking of moral statements as true or false.

This, and more complex considerations as well, have counted heavily in favor of the "no truth" account of moral discourse. But there are difficulties here as well. Even if, as with descriptive statements, there are no facts that moral statements simply describe—even if there is nothing like ' " 'The cat is on the mat' is true" if and only if the cat is on the mat'—it does not follow that it is not proper to say that statements of logically diverse kinds are true. Mathematical and logical statements are true; more generally there are analytic truths even though such a "correspondence theory" will not begin to work for them. Just as we recognize factual truths and logical truths, why cannot we recognize moral truths as well?

It is here where the good reasons approach and Kurt Baier's analysis in particular can be of considerable help. Baier thinks he has a way around our problem. His first move is indirect. It consists (1) in showing how we determine the truth of claims about what is legal or customary, and (2) in showing how very different moral concepts are from legal concepts or from mere customs. To find out whether it is true that it is illegal for Caucasians and Negroes to marry in Mississippi, we need only to find out what the law is in Mississippi and how this bears on U.S. Federal laws; to find out whether it is customary for white men to flirt with Negro girls in Mississippi, we need only determine what the practice is in Mississippi. Once we discover what the law is or what the custom is, we have unequivocally settled the question of the truth of our legal claim or our claim about what is customary. But this is not so with moral questions. If we make a moral claim, if we assert "It is immoral to prevent Caucasians and Negroes from marrying in Mississippi or anyplace else" or "It is wrong for white men to flirt with Negro girls when they cannot marry them, have no intention of marrying them, and do not even treat them as persons," the truth or falsity of these claims is *not* decided and cannot be decided simply by discovering what are the moral convictions of the group. Morality differs radically from law and custom here. If I know what is demanded or prohibited by the moral code of my society, I do *not* thereby know what is right in my society or elsewhere. Once a person knows what the law or custom of his own or some other culture is, he cannot intelligibly ask whether his convictions about what is legal or customary in *that culture* are true, but this is not so for morality. How then do we determine whether a moral conviction is true?

Baier's answer is very simple: "Our moral convictions are true if they can be seen to be required or acceptable from the moral point of view."[4] When we say that a moral judgment is true we endorse that judgment; we endorse it as a judgment that is rationally warranted; and when the judgment in question is a moral judgment, to say that it is rationally warranted comes to acknowledging it as acceptable from the moral point of view.

But what is it for something to be acceptable from the moral point of view? What is it to take the moral point of view? In Chapter 8 of his *The Moral Point of View*, Baier explicates what it is to take "the moral point of view." To take the moral point of view, three conditions must be satisfied.

1. We must adopt rules of conduct not as rules of thumb designed to promote our own individual interests, but as matters of principle. As Baier points out, "this involves conforming to the rules whether or not doing so favors one's own or anyone else's aim."[5]

2. A moral agent must adopt rules to which not only he and his friends conform as a matter of principle, but rules to which everyone can conform as a matter of principle. Moral rules are meant for everybody.[6]
There are four subsidiary conditions which need to be noted under this condition.

   a. It must be possible to teach a moral rule to everybody.
   b. It must be a rule such that its purpose would not be defeated if everyone acted on it.
   c. It must be a rule such that it would not be defeated if a person let it be known that he adopted it.
   d. It must not be a rule such that it would be literally impossible for everyone to act in accordance with it.

3. Moral rules must be rules which are adopted for the good of everyone alike. The principle of impartiality or justice is involved here, since the interests of all people must be furthered, or at least given equal consideration when some moral rule has to be overridden. Baier gives us a case to make clear exactly what it is that he means. This condition excludes from morality any set of rules "which enrich the ruling class

---

[4] Kurt Baier, *The Moral Point of View* (Ithaca, New York, 1958), pp. 183-184. In my "History of Ethics," vol. III, *Encyclopedia of Philosophy*, ed. by Paul Edwards (New York, 1957), pp. 109-112, I have given a general characterization of the good reasons approach and tried to place it in contemporary ethical theory.

[5] Kurt Baier, *op. cit.*, p. 191.

[6] *Ibid.*, p. 195.

at the expense of the masses."⁷ It excludes any rule that is not reversible. This is to say, the behaviour in question "must be acceptable to a person whether he is at the 'giving' or 'receiving' end of it."⁸

One further point is important in considering what it is to take the moral point of view. When one takes the moral point of view one must, when one has a specific moral perplexity, review the *facts* in the light of one's moral convictions.⁹ The important thing to see here is that if one is reasoning morally, one must attend to the facts relevant to the case.

According to Baier, we can determine true from false moral statements by determining which statements are *acceptable* from the moral point of view. If a statement is acceptable from the moral point of view, it is true; if not, not. Only certain rules of conduct will satisfy these conditions. This means that no moral statement can be true unless it is made in accordance with and acceptable from the point of view of those norms which incapsulate the moral point of view.

This view, if correct, would give us some moral truths, some knowledge of good and evil. But Baier's view and the good reasons approach generally has not escaped thorough criticism. It has been thought by many in some way to enshrine, as *the* logic of moral discourse, the rather limited moral views of some particular men at a particular time and place. Paul Taylor has made this reaction specific and penetrating in his striking article "The Ethnocentric Fallacy."¹⁰ Taylor argues that Baier's effort is reduced in essence to the claim that a moral claim is true only if it is made in accordance with the moral principles of liberal Western society, but these principles in turn are not testable—nothing establishes their truth or falsity. But to argue in this way—to argue as Baier does—is, Taylor argues, to commit the ethnocentric fallacy.

Let me explain exactly what Taylor means when he makes this claim. Baier, Taylor argues, defines "the moral point of view" in terms of the moral code of liberal Western Society.

> As a logical consequence of his definition, all moral convictions which do not accord with those of that particular society are false. But this assumes that one set of moral convictions are true, and does not tell us how we know *this*. In fact, by making moral knowledge relative to or dependent upon these convictions, it places the convictions themselves beyond truth and falsity and hence renders them arbitrary.¹¹

---

⁷ *Ibid.*, p. 201.
⁸ *Ibid.*, p. 202.
⁹ *Ibid.*, p. 185.
¹⁰ Paul Taylor, "The Ethnocentric Fallacy," *The Monist*, vol. 47 (1963), pp. 563–584.
¹¹ *Ibid.*, p. 565.

This challenge of Taylor's is a powerful one—a challenge that cannot in some form or other but occur to any thoughtful reader of Baier's book. Let us take a close look at Taylor's incisive arguments.

Taylor points out that "if we define the word 'moral' in terms of an impartial set of rules, according to which no act is right unless reversible, then it becomes *self-contradictory* to talk of the moral code of a society which, for example, places women in a subordinate position to men."[12] But if we adopt this definition, we in effect make the truth of someone's moral convictions "relative to the moral code of what might be dubbed 'liberal Western society'—the society which had adopted a moral code embodying principles of justice, impartiality, and brotherhood extending to all human beings."[13] At this point Taylor drives home his most crucial point. For all his sophistication, Baier has been very culture-bound, very ethnocentric in his characterization of the moral point of view. Taylor remarks that the above liberal code of conduct

> . . . is only one among many. However deeply our own conscience and moral outlook may have been shaped by it, we must recognize that other societies in the history of the world have been able to function on the basis of other codes. There are societies with caste systems, societies which practice slavery, societies in which women are treated as inferior to men and so on. To claim that a person who is a member of one of those societies and who knows its moral code, nevertheless does not have true moral convictions is, it seems to me, fundamentally correct. But such a claim cannot be justified on the ground of Baier's concept of the moral point of view, for that is to assume that the moral code of liberal Western society is the only genuine morality. This renders it nonsensical to talk about alternative moral codes, unless we place "moral" in brackets or quotation marks . . . to indicate that such codes are somehow alleged to be moral but are not genuinely so.[14]

To proceed in this ethnocentric way, Taylor argues, produces the very reverse effect of what Baier was after. Baier wanted to show how one could correctly assert that the moral convictions of a society, including his own, could be false. But given this ethnocentric definition of "the moral point of view" and given Baier's definition of "moral truth," moral truth comes to depend on which codes of which societies are referred to. If a moral claim is acceptable from the point of view of Western liberal morality, it is true; if not, it is false. This is a perfect rationalization for ethnocentrism. Moreover, it will now become senseless to ask whether a person's moral

---

[12] *Ibid.*, pp. 568–569.
[13] *Ibid.*, p. 570.
[14] *Ibid.*

convictions are true if they are acceptable from the point of view of liberal Western morality. But this is itself, Taylor argues, surely nonsense for if this were so (1) "Act *x* is forbidden by the moral code of society *S*, but is it really wrong?" would become equivalent to (2) "Act *x* is forbidden by the moral code of society *S*, but is it forbidden by the moral code of liberal Western society?" But the two questions are not equivalent. (2) could be settled in the way we settle questions of what is customary or what is legal, but, as Baier has shown himself, we do not and cannot settle moral questions in this way. Furthermore (1) would make sense when asked of any society, but (2) does not make sense when society *S* is liberal Western society. Thus (1) and (2) are very different questions.

Surely Taylor is right *if* to take the "moral point of view" is to take a point of view wherein we must, to be even *reasoning morally*, have the ideal of the brotherhood of all men. There have been plenty of societies that have had moral codes that did not even remotely have this ideal. As Westermarck points out,

> Primitive peoples carefully distinguish between an act of homicide committed within their own community and one where the victim is a stranger: while the former is in ordinary circumstances disapproved of, the latter is in most cases allowed and often considered worthy of praise. And the same holds true of theft and lying and the infliction of other injuries. Apart from the privileges granted to guests, which are always of very short duration, a stranger is in early society devoid of all rights.[15]

Westermarck, utilizing a wealth of empirical material, goes on to show how in Greek society, Roman society, among the early Teutonic groups, through the Middle Ages and down into the seventeenth century in Europe, similar moral conceptions were very widespread. Even today, Westermarck points out, such ideas are not entirely dead within Western culture. Modern moral philosophers argue against it, but such tribal moral beliefs—beliefs which come to the fore during wartime and in times of political and economic pressure—are surely not dead among us. As normative ethicists, as moralists, we may surely deplore such "moralities" and seek to argue for a universalistic morality in which the ideal of brotherhood and beneficence is extended to all men, but plainly such alternative moral codes and moral conceptions do exist.

Certainly this is a powerful attack. In a very plain sense of "adopted for the good of everyone alike" not all rules that as a matter of linguistic propriety can be properly called "moral rules" or "moral principles" enshrine such an intent.

[15] Edward Westermarck, *Ethical Relativity* (London, 1932), p. 197.

Yet this is not the whole tale. What Baier says about the third condition for the moral point of view, perhaps with a little stretching in the direction of Hare, can be *interpreted* in a way that does not fall prey to the ethnocentric fallacy.

A key to what I want to claim here lies in Baier's Kantian claim that moral judgments must be reversible. When we say that a moral claim must be reversible, we are saying that whatever is to count as "a moral claim" must be acceptable to the agent whether he is on the giving or receiving end of it. Now it has been argued that this reversibility is not analytically linked with what it is for something to count as "a moral statement." After all, people have said, "Women should not vote," "Black men should not live in the same apartment blocks as white men," "The ruling classes have a right to enrich themselves at the expense of the masses," "Germans deserve one kind of treatment, Jews another," "People who are shipwrecked may be plundered." But, it has been argued, clearly non-reversible and neanderthal though they be, that these judgments are unequivocally moral judgments. It is, Taylor and others have argued, not a necessary condition for something's being a moral judgment that it be reversible. In thinking that it is, so the argument runs, Baier and Kant reveal an ethnocentric understanding of morality.

I want to argue that these examples not withstanding, reversibility *is* such a necessary condition and this Kantian claim, *properly understood*, does not commit us to an ethnocentric view of morality. There remains a very crucial sense in morals—in which even people who hold such apparently non-reversible views as the anti-Femininist, the racist and the Nazi quoted above, if they are reasoning morally at all, must be applying the criterion of reversibility. Consider this snatch of a dialogue:

A: Women should not vote. They must always remain in a subordinate place in our society.

B: If you were a woman you wouldn't say that.

A: No indeed I wouldn't. I would be quite justified in maintaining that if I were a woman I would have the right to vote, but I still would say that other women ought not to vote.

B: But then it isn't "being a woman" that should disqualify one from voting, but "being a certain kind of a person." There is something about *you* that entitles you, whether you are or are not a woman, to vote and the women whom you say should not vote lack that quality.

A: No, I'm not saying anything of the kind. There is—I confess —nothing distinctive about me. I am just saying that women *ought* not to vote. But I am *not* at all willing to say that if I were a woman, in all relevant respects like the women whom I say should not vote, that then *I* should not vote.

When *A* replies in this way he is saying something that is not intelligible as a bit of moral or normative discourse. It is in this sense that reversibility is a necessary requirement of the moral point of view. But such a limitation does not make it self-contradictory, as Taylor thinks, to set forth a moral code that places women in a subordinate position to men. Neanderthals who so argue will come up with some spurious factual claim that women are somehow either naturally or, as a matter of sociological fact, inferior to men and cannot therefore be given the responsibility of voting. But if such a man is reasoning morally, he must—logically must—be prepared to admit that if he were a woman or were inferior in the same specified way, then he too ought not to be allowed to vote. If he is not prepared to so reason, we would not *understand* what he could mean by saying that he was making a *moral* claim. He would not be playing the moral language game. He would not be thinking as a moral agent. The same thing can be said for the other examples I gave. They do not count against the contention that moral judgments must be reversible. This requirement of reversibility is but a facet of universalizability or the generalization principle, a principle that Taylor himself takes to be analytically tied to anything that could count as a normative judgment.[16] It is, Taylor rightly argues, analytic to "say that whatever is right or wrong for one person is right or wrong for every similar person in similar circumstances." In this sense all normative judgments and *a fortiori* all moral judgments must be reversible, and in *that sense*, impartial. As moral agents, we must be committed to such an idea of impartiality.

Yet we must not forget what both Hare and Taylor have stressed, that this requirement *by itself* does not determine the *content* of any moral judgment. It does not, by itself, block a tribal morality. Greeks can (and have) said of Barbarians that they ought not to have the rights of Greeks; Germans can (and have) said of Jews that they do not have the rights of Germans. But to say this, and make their remarks intelligible as moral remarks, they must contend that there is something about Barbarians or Jews that makes them different from Greeks and Germans.

[16] Paul Taylor, *op. cit.*, pp. 575–576.

But, as Westermarck and more recently Hare have recognized, once we dwell on and take to heart this generalizing feature of moral discourse, it becomes very difficult—if we are at all clear-headed—to be a tribalist in ethics, for if Barbarians, Jews, Negroes, women, the proletariat, and the like are not to have the treatment the tribalist claims for himself, there must—logically must—be something about them that justifies that difference in treatment. That is, there must be something that the maker of the moral judgment would acknowledge as justifying a like treatment for him if that characteristic could be correctly attributed to him. It takes a very fanatical and irrational German to be prepared—to really be prepared—to put himself and all his family into the concentration camp if it turns out that they are Jews. We could play the little trick on him Hare proposes. First, by forged documents we get him to believe that he really is what the Nazis would call a Jew and then, if in true fanatical fashion he agrees that he and his family should have a first-class ticket to the gas chambers, we prove to him that the documents are forged and then ask him, what reason he has for claiming in the first place that he and his family should be gassed and why moments later he has changed his mind. What has changed about him and his family that justifies freeing them from this torment? Does he really see or notice anything about his family and children or about his own person in the two different situations that would justify a switch in treatment? He can, of course, continue to say that it is their "Jewishness/non-Jewishness" that justifies the switch in treatment, but then he is really caught up in obscurantism and mystagogy, for our very trick has shown that there is nothing empirically detectable about being a Jew that is relevant to his moral claim. Perhaps Jewishness is a non-natural intuitable, toti-resultant quality supervening on all Jews and only on Jews.

In sum, I have tried to argue, as against Taylor, that Baier's characterization of the moral point of view can be interpreted in such a way that it does not commit the ethnocentric fallacy. I have, as Taylor has, concentrated on Baier's third condition, but now I shall show that the first two conditions do not commit Baier to identifying morality with liberal Western morality and that the three conditions, taken in conjunction with Baier's claim that in reasoning morally we must attend to the facts, give us adequate criteria for deciding when a moral judgment is true.

Let us consider Baier's second condition, namely his contention that a rule, to count as a "moral rule," must be one to which everyone can conform and a rule must be meant for everybody. Our prior discussion should have made it evident that condition two is plausible only under a rather distinctive interpretation. That is, we have to give a distinctive reading of "rule meant for everybody" or "rule to which everyone can conform as a matter of principle." My above remarks about reversibility make it plain how and in what way moral rules are meant for everybody and are rules to which one can conform as a matter of principle. If something is a moral rule it must apply to like people in like circumstances. If it is all right for a starving Brazilian farmer to steal in order to keep alive, if he can't get the means of life in any other way, then it would be all right for anyone like this farmer and in the same kind of situation to steal. In that way, and without ethnocentrism, moral rules are for everyone. But this does not commit us to the absurdity that psychotics and mentally defective people can conform to them, but only to claiming that if, and when, such people can act as moral agents, then they too must, in the relevant circumstances, act in certain prescribed ways.

If a "rule" to have the logical status of "a moral rule" must be universalizable in the manner I have described, it clearly must be a rule that can be taught to anyone capable of moral agency to whom the moral rule correctly applies. If a moral rule applies to men of a certain sort, distinctively situated, this commits us to the assertion that when certain conditions obtain they ought to do what the rule enjoins; and this, in turn, implies that they can do it. But surely a necessary condition for their following the rule is that they understand it. Thus the moral rule must be teachable to the men to whom it correctly applies. But in specifying these men we must specify them by pointing to the fact that they have certain determinate characteristics, and *universalizability* commits us to saying that the moral rule in question must apply to anyone who has these characteristics. This would hold for anything recognizable as "a moral rule." This is a plausible, if somewhat reduced, reading of Baier's claim that a moral rule must be teachable to everybody. I am saying rather that it must be capable of being taught to everyone to whom it can be correctly applied.

Baier's first condition poses more difficulties. Some have thought that there are, or at least can be, "egoistic moralities," but Baier tells us that to adopt the moral point of view is to conform to rules whether or not conforming to them promotes our self-interest. If something counts as a "moral rule" or as a "moral claim" it must (and the force of the "must" here is logical) override self-interest.

That this is so and why it is so is plain enough when we think of the *raison d'être* or, more modestly and more appropriately, a central *raison d'être*, for having a moral code—*any* moral code at all. Any society needs some device for impartially adjudicating conflicts of interest. Society is necessary for human beings, and when human beings live together, band together in a society with at least the minimal cooperation this implies, they will have conflicts of interest. If, when such conflicts occur, each man were to seek to further his self-interest alone, there would be the kind of conflict and chaos in society that no reasonable man could desire. In fact, if men were to act in this way, it would not even be correct to speak of them as living together in society. Thus to live together, to further one of the main ends of morality, men must adopt rules which override self-interest. To take the moral point of view of necessity involves conforming to such rules. But to conform to such rules is not simply to commit oneself to liberal Western morality. It is rather to adopt a point of view that is and must be implicit in all moral reasoning.

We are not out of the dark woods yet. Granting that moral judgments must be universalizable, granting that in the sense specified they must be for the good of everyone alike, we still do not know and cannot determine *what* is for the good of everyone alike, until we can determine something of the content of "for the good of everyone alike." Until we can do this we can hardly be said to have any knowledge of good and evil or any moral truth.

What is it for something to be for the *good* of everyone alike or even for something to be good for me or good period? If we leave the content of "good" unspecified in stating the moral point of view, then if two moralists both adopt the moral point of view and make logically incompatible moral judgments both of which are—under these circumstances—acceptable from the moral point of view, because they both satisfy Baier's three conditions, then we would have two logically incompatible moral judgments both of which, according to Baier's specifications, would be true. But it is a self-contradiction to assert that two logically incompatible assertions could both be true. Baier would surely add, but, of course, two mutually incompatible statements cannot be true, but the problem remains that if we accept his explication of "moral truth" there is no possible way of determining which of the two mutually incompatible moral statements are true.

An example may make my claim clearer. Suppose *A* claims that wives ought not to have lunch alone with men who are not their husbands, and *B* claims that this is absurdly medieval, that it is perfectly all right for a woman to have lunch alone with a man who is not her husband. Now these two judgments are both moral judgments, both satisfy Baier's three conditions and they are logically incompatible. We should want to say that they both can't be true, but given Baier's account, as explicated above, we could not possibly say which moral statement was true.

The way out here is to realize that in characterizing the moral point of view, we must *not* speak of "the good of everyone alike" in such a way that "good" is used so that it can have *just any* content. But when we claim "good" must have a certain content, we again run the risk of committing the ethnocentric fallacy. It is tempting to argue that in adopting the moral point of view, we attribute a certain content to "good" but not everyone would use "good" in this way; there are, as J. O. Urmson argues, alternative and often conflicting criteria for "good." But we must—if we follow Baier—specify moral truth with reference to the moral point of view and here we find that once we consider "good-making criteria," we get a relativity in the very specification of the moral point of view that defeats Baier's claim that we can develop an objective test for the truth of moral statements.

The question I want to ask here is this: Are the "good-making criteria" used in such moral appraisals all *that* relative? When we are trying to develop a rational criterion for deciding whether certain actions, rules or practices are good or bad, we are concerned with whether they are, more than any of their alternatives, in the best interests of everyone; and in talking of the best interests of everyone, we are talking about their most extensive welfare and well-being. Now, if you like, you may call "general welfare" and "human well-being" grading labels or evaluative terms or prescriptive terms or normative terms or what you will, but they are, all the same, so tied to certain descriptive criteria that actions, rules or practices which did not satisfy these criteria could not be properly said to be in the general welfare or to serve the human well-being.[17] Practices or rules which sanctioned starving everyone to the point where the human animal could just barely keep alive, prohibited all sexual relations, constantly interrupted people's sleep to the point where they were just capable of keeping alive, made both play and work impossible and destroyed all human affection, could not possibly be correctly said to be in the

[17] In this context see also my "Appraising Doing the Thing Done," *The Journal of Philosophy*, vol. 57 (1960); "Progress," *The Lock Haven Review*, no. 7 (1965); "On Looking Back at the Emotive Theory," *Methodos*, vol. 14 (1962); and "Problems of Ethics," vol. III, *Encyclopedia of Philosophy*, ed. by Paul Edwards (New York, 1967), pp. 130–132.

general welfare and serve human well-being. And if they could not serve human well-being or be in the general welfare they could not be in the best interests of everyone and if they could not be in the best interests of everyone they could not be for the good of everyone alike and if they could not be for the good of everyone alike they could not be compatible with the moral point of view.

Such criteria give content to the moral point of view and make it impossible for both the judgments of A and B to be true. Furthermore, while such an explication of "for the good of everyone alike" *may* commit what has been called the "naturalistic fallacy," it does not commit the "ethnocentric fallacy." To accept such criteria about human welfare or human well-being does not commit us to liberal Western morality or even to Western morality, it is part of *any* morality.

It could be argued that what I have said above is mistaken; such a conception of "general welfare" or "human well-being" is still ethnocentric, for Buddhists striving after nirvana and Plains Indians on the vision quest regard certain forms of behavior as supremely desirable even though they run contrary to what I have said is in the general welfare or for human well-being. After all, we can have an "ethic of renunciation." Someone with such an ethic, it is natural to argue, would have a concept of the general welfare very different from the one just put before you. As such ascetics conceive of man's deepest well-being and welfare, we have something that sharply conflicts with what I have said. Such renunciation, they would argue, in reality serves men's deepest well-being and is for the general welfare. "General welfare" and "human well-being" are essentially contested concepts.

This objection to my argument will not do. It will not show that my criterion is ethnocentric, for such behavior was never advocated as a basis for social action or as a way of life for *all* Buddhists or *all* Plains Indians to adopt. It was prescribed for the holy man and not for the ordinary Plains Indian or the ordinary Buddhist. Such behavior did not, even for the holy man, serve as criteria for what was for *human* well-being or in the *general* welfare. Here their criteria overlap with the criteria used by what Taylor calls "liberal Western morality"; and the overlap includes the criteria I gave. There is no good reason to think such criteria are ethnocentric.

There is a further consideration that deserves attention here. As we noted before, in adopting the moral point of view, we are committed, when we are able to review the facts carefully, to clarifying these facts for ourselves before making decisions, advocatig certainn moral rules, or supporting certain moral practices. Now where there *seems* to be some alteration or qualification of the criteria for human well-being that I have offered, it has been in the service of some superstitious, ideological, or wildly metaphysical scheme. That nirvana can be attained, that there is a numinosity answering to the Indian's quest, is either false or without factual significance.[18] Attention to the facts, including the understanding we would achieve if we attained even a minimum of conceptual clarity, would lead us to reject such seeming alterations and qualifications of Baier's characterization of the moral point of view. To carry out moral reasoning fully, we must attend carefully to the non-moral facts and we must seek to be clear-headed. If we are clear-headed and do attend to the facts, we will not go on the vision quest or seek or even expect to attain nirvana.

We must also note that moral judgments are judgments that are ideally made in the light of a full knowledge of the relevant facts and they must, logically must, be made in the light of the facts that it is reasonable to expect the moral agent to have in his possession when he must make his moral decision or render judgment. To take the moral point of view is to reason in this way and it is to use "good" in the relevant contexts with this factual content. Since this is so, it cannot be the case that two logically incompatible moral judgments, like *A*'s and *B*'s about wives' dining with men who are not their husbands, could both be acceptable from the moral point of view. They have different consequences for human well-being and, everything being equal, if *A*'s judgment is such that it would, if followed, make for greater general welfare than *B*'s, then only *A*'s judgment is acceptable from the moral point of view; and, if there are no other alternatives acceptable from the moral point of view here, then *A*'s judgment is required from the moral pont of view and *a fortiori* true.

The concept of good is sufficiently vague and moral reasoning is sufficiently complex to make it the case that for a wide and important range of cases, we cannot determine what we ought to do with any objectivity. But there are also standard cases and contexts in which we can determine moral truth—that is, we can determine how we ought to act from the moral point of view. Moreover, given a sophisticated and a determined application of moral reasoning

---

[18] My remark here may seem brusque and dogmatic, but I could hardly develop my arguments for it here, though I have in some detail in my "On Speaking of God," *Theoria*, vol. 28 (1962), Part 2; "Religious Perplexity and Faith," *The Crane Review*, vol. 8 (1965); "God-Talk," *Sophia*, vol. 3 (1964); "On Fixing the Reference Range of 'God'," *Religious Studies*, vol. 2 (1966); and in my book *The Quest for God* (forthcoming).

and an extensive knowledge of man and his world, our knowledge of good and evil can constantly expand. The concept of truth has an application in morals and we have definite ways of determining truth in morality.

New York University

II

On Ethical Egoism

JESSE KALIN*

[An ethical egoist can admit that] if a certain experience or disposition of his is good, a precisely similar experience or disposition of *B*'s will be also and equally good. But he will assert that it is not his duty to produce good experiences and dispositions as such, without regard to the question of who will have them. *A* has an obligation to produce good experiences and dispositions in *himself*, and no such direct obligation to produce them in *B* or in anyone else. *A* recognizes that *B* has no such direct obligation to produce them in *A* or in anyone else [except himself]. This doctrine does not contradict itself in any way.[1]

Consider the following exchange between an (ethical) egoist *E* and a non-egoistic opponent *G*:

G: Why did you steal my plans and force me out of business?
E: Why not? Those plans enabled my company to survive and it's growing. In addition, I made a big profit which I would otherwise have lost.
G: But don't you know that stealing is immoral, and wrong?
E: Why?
G: How would you like it if I had stolen your plans?
E: That would have been the breaks of the game.

If *E* were a philosopher, he might have said the following:

(a) It is morally permissible for me to pursue my self-interest even when it conflicts with the interests of others.

or a stronger claim:

(b) I ought to pursue my self-interest above all else.

G can rightly point out that *E* cannot stop with this, but must proceed to universalize (a) and (b) to something like:

---

* I wish to thank my colleagues who discussed this paper with me, particularly Professor Thomas Nagel and Mr. Fred Berger.
[1] C. D. Broad, "Certain Features in Moore's Ethical Doctrines" in Paul Schlipp (ed.), *The Philosophy of G. E. Moore* (Chicago, 1942), pp. 44-45.

(*a'*) It is morally permissible for everyone to pursue his self-interest even when it conflicts with the interests of others.
(*b'*) Everyone ought to pursue his self-interest above all else.

Why universalization? E is claiming at least that there are no moral reasons overriding his position and perhaps also that he has strong moral reasons supporting it. If he does have such reasons, anyone in a similar situation will have the same reasons. In this particular case, it is plausible to argue that everyone is in a similar situation—that of having self-interests (prudential interests)—and hence for (*a*) or (*b*) to be correct, a universalized form of them must also be correct.

It is at this point that many philosophers have tried to stop the egoist by claiming that (*a'*) and (*b'*) are unsound, that, hence, because they are therefore not even possible moral principles, they cannot be appealed to by the egoist and that, consequently, *ethical* egoism is not possible. Among these philosophers accepting some form of universalization as a necessary feature of any moral principle, there has been wide disagreement concerning this claim. Sidgwick (in *The Methods of Ethics*), Broad, and Moore,[2] for instance, have thought egoism sound in this respect while, among many others, Kant, Kurt Baier, Brian Medlin (all of whom will be discussed below) and also Frankena[3] and Brandt[4] have disagreed or tended to disagree. In the following sections, I shall examine three attempts to show ethical egoism unsound and shall argue that they fail. I shall then examine a further attempt which also fails, and finally, I shall remark on the implications of these failures for moral philosophy.

I

Ethical egoism is the view that everyone ought to pursue his own self-interest (happiness, well-being) in preference to the self-interest of anyone else. The point people normally have in mind in accepting and advocating this ethical principle is that of giving their own interests a moral sanction by justifying their self-interested behavior in terms of a universalized rule. By doing so they are no longer open to the charge that they are making exceptions in their own favor; they are allowing themselves nothing more than is allowed—morally—to anyone else. The egoist does not claim to be acting merely prudently; his claim is that prudence is always moral,

---
[2] G. E. Moore, *Ethics* (London, 1912), p. 143. Moore also thinks that ethical egoism is false.
[3] William Frankena, *Ethics* (Englewood Cliffs, 1963), pp. 16–18.
[4] Richard Brandt, *Ethical Theory* (Englewood Cliffs, 1959), ch. 14.

i.e., right; prudence is one's duty; prudential reasons are always decisive in answering the question "What ought I to do?"

There are several possible formulations of ethical egoism; I shall consider the following as the most plausible and defensible, and it will be the subject of the following discussion:

(i) $(\forall x)(\forall y)$ (x ought to do y iff y is in x's [overall] self-interest).

(i) is a formalization of (b'). In this paper I shall not consider (a'), confining my attention to the stronger position. In this section I shall examine the following three kinds of criticism derived from the following two considerations:

First, since a general moral rule (containing "ought" or "right") is prescriptive in character, it must be possible to employ consistently the rule to evaluate and prescribe (or determine) both my own actions and the actions of others. Objections (A) and (B) derive from this consideration:

(A) Ethical egoism fails to provide a decision procedure for acting.

(B) Ethical egoism makes moral assessment impossible; in particular, it commits the egoist to contradictory moral judgments.

This brings me to the second consideration. Consistency, both between one's beliefs and between one's beliefs and one's actions, is a rational requirement. Objection (C) derives from this consideration:

(C) The ethical egoist must be "practically inconsistent."

II

In his article, "Ultimate Principles and Ethical Egoism," Brian Medlin claims that ethical egoism is the expression of inconsistent desires and that this feature prevents it from fulfilling the role required of ultimate ethical principles, namely, that of guiding our actions, telling us what to do, and determining our choice between alternatives.[5]

Medlin gives the following as more or less equivalent formulations of ethical egoism:

---

[5] Brian Medlin, "Ultimate Principles and Ethical Egoism," *The Australasian Journal of Philosophy*, vol. 35 (1957), pp. 111–118; reprinted in Richard Brandt (ed.), *Value and Obligation* (New York, 1961), pp. 150–157. References are to the reprint in Brandt.

(ii) "Everyone should observe his own interests regardless of the interests of others" (p. 154),
(iii) "Let each man do what he wants regardless of what anyone else wants" (p. 155), and
(iv) "Let each man do what he wants and let each man disregard what others want when their desires clash with his own" (p. 155).

His main argument against ethical egoism is the following: An essential feature of an ethical principle is that it guides conduct. It does this by expressing the attitudes, desires, and purposes setting the ends that guide action. But egoism expresses not one coherent set of ends but rather contrary ends. In effect, the agent is told to do each of several incompatible actions and hence not told to do anything at all. Thus egoism fails as a possible principle of conduct.

Medlin argues[6] for the minor premiss—inconsistent desires (ends of action) are expressed by ethical egoism as a principle—by showing which desires the principle expresses. Thus the egoist seems to be saying: "I want myself to come out on top and *I don't care about Tom, Dick, Harry, . . .*" and "I want Tom to come out on top and *I don't care about myself, Dick, Harry, . . .*" It is not exactly clear how the desires in italics are inconsistent with those of the rest of the statement. Does the principle say something so blatant as "Do care about Tom and don't care about Tom" or something subtle such as "Tom should come out on top, if he can do so"? It is inconsistent to want everyone to come out "on top," since only one person can do so. But the ethical egoist need not be wanting this. Rather, cannot (ii)–(iv) be expressing desires such as:

I want A to behave in such and such a manner, and
I want B to behave in such and such a manner, and
I want C to behave in such and such a manner, and . . . ,

this manner being to employ the following decision procedure (maxim) for their actions: "I should do y iff y satisfies my (overall) interests." Thus a more formal expression of ethical egoism would be:

(i) $(\forall x)(\forall y)$ (x ought to do y iff y is in x's [overall] self-interest).

This thesis seems to express a consistent set of desires (to use Medlin's terminology). The fact that, if people were to behave this way they would conflict, does not make my desire that they so

[6] B. Medlin in *Value and Obligation, op. cit.*, p 154.

behave inconsistent. To desire that people behave selfishly is not to desire that any one of them come out on top; nor is it to desire that oneself come out on top; it is simply to desire a particular, possible state of affairs, namely, that each person follows a particular rule ("desire" is a strong term; one can substitute "consider right" or "consider morally obligatory"). Notice that this interpretation seems closer to the sense of the quotation from Broad. For instance, Broad makes no appeal to "everyone coming out on top" as the set of ends desired by the ethical egoist. Secondly, and more important, even if (i) were still to express inconsistent desires, it provides every agent with a workable decision procedure: each person is to do what is most in his self-interest. (It does not tell us how to figure this out, but isn't that a different problem?). Thus, I conclude that this argument against ethical egoism—that it cannot serve as a guide of conduct—fails.[7]

III

In his book *The Moral Point of View*,[8] Kurt Baier wishes to hold that even enlightened egoism cannot be a moral principle since "those who adopt consistent egoism cannot make moral judgments. Moral talk is impossible for consistent egoists. But this amounts to a *reductio ad absurdum* of consistent egoism" (p. 95). I take Baier's argument in this passage to be the following: If the ethical egoist is going to make moral evaluations of people's behavior at all, he will be committed to holding contradictory evaluations of the same act; his only alternative is to hold that moral evaluation is inappropriate to a wide spectrum of action to which it is obviously appropriate even on his own principle; in either case the consequences of ethical egoism are absurd. Baier considers the following example:

B and K both seek the presidency of Q. It is in B's (overall) self-interest to become president and to eliminate K afterwards; similarly, it is in K's (overall) self-interest to become president and to eliminate B afterwards. Of course, there can be only one president. Furthermore, in the light of this it would be in B's interest to assassinate K, and it would be in K's interest to prevent B from assassinating him. Thus those actions in B's self-interest are decidedly against the self-interest of K; and *vice versa*. Baier thinks that from this it follows on

---

[7] Medlin also advances an argument like the one given in Sect. VI of this paper. What is interesting about it is that Medlin seems to think egoism could be a secondary moral principle instrumental to some other end, yet in the argument I have given he claims that it cannot be a moral principle at all.

[8] Kurt Baier, *The Moral Point of View*, abridged edition (New York, 1965), ch. 5, particularly Sect. 3 (cf. ch. 8, Sect. 1 in the first edition [Ithaca, 1958]).

ethical egoism that the same act will be both right and wrong. Let K prevent B from assassinating him, and let us call this action 'a'. Since a is definitely in K's self-interest, it is right and what K ought to do. But a is also wrong, for in preventing the assassination, K has prevented B from doing what is right and what B ought to do, and surely it is wrong to prevent someone from doing what is his (moral) duty. Therefore, a is both right and wrong. "But one and the same act (logically) cannot be both morally wrong and not morally wrong. Hence in cases like these no moral judgments apply" which is absurd (p. 95).

One should note immediately that the egoist is committed to contradictory judgments, and hence to absurdity, only if an additional premiss, which Baier takes to be self-evident, is added to (i), namely:

(v) One ought never to prevent someone from doing what he ought to do, or

(v') It is always wrong to prevent someone from doing what is right.

Neither version of (v) seems to be true, and I shall discuss them below.

On the basis of (i) alone, therefore, no contradictions follow. However, there are some formulations of ethical egoism which do yield contradictory judgments without a version of (v), for example[9]:

(vi) An action x is right (ought to be done) iff it is in the speaker's (critic's) self-interest (the speaker may or may not also be the agent). (Or perhaps: An action is right iff it is in *my* self-interest.)

(vii) Someone ought to do some action iff that action is in the speaker's (critic's) self-interest. (Or perhaps: x ought to do y iff y is in *my* self-interest.)

Thus in (vi) it will be the case that a—K's prevention of B's assassination of K—is *both* right and wrong, that a both ought and ought not to have been done, for from K's point of view it follows that a is right since a is in K's interest, and from B's point of view it follows that a is wrong since a is contrary to B's interest. On these formulations moral judgments have lost all objectivity and the egoist is committed to a peculiar usage of moral terms. But the egoist need not go to these extremes to maintain the justness of his position for (i) does not have these faults. On (i) all that follows is that K ought

[9] Frankena, for example, takes ethical egoism in the sense of (vi) and (vii). *Op. cit.*, pp. 16-17.

to do *a* and that, therefore, *a* is right and that *B* ought to do something else, *b*, and that this too is right. Both *B* and *K* must agree to this, and without presupposing (v) they, in particular *B*, have no basis for saying that *a* is wrong even though it is not in *B*'s self-interest. There is simply no substitution instance (or point of view) for (i) on which it follows that *K* ought not to do *a* or that *a* is wrong. Thus Baier has not yet shown moral talk to be impossible for the consistent egoist; the egoist need only abandon (vi) [or (vii)] for (i) and in addition deny (v).

IV

The success of this defense against Baier depends upon the falsity of (v), but before examining that premiss I wish to consider a third attempt to refute egoism which is similar to Baier's and which similarly depends upon a version of (v). Baier has argued that ethical egoism commits its holder to a formal contradiction, i.e., to holding contradictory beliefs. The correlate to this attack is the view that ethical egoism also commits its holder to what can be called a *practical contradiction*, to being forced always to act contrary to one of his moral beliefs.

A man may be criticized on grounds of inconsistency not only when his beliefs are incompatible or self-contradictory, but also when his actions go against his beliefs. This can occur in a variety of ways and frequently we take such behavior as evidence of his hypocrisy, insincerity, self-deception, his having changed his mind, or simply of his "not really believing that such and such." At the least we normally require from him some further explanation, some further reasons justifying or excusing his action or else qualifying his belief; lacking such, he should either give up his beliefs or renounce his action. This kind of inconsistency appears necessarily to characterize the egoist; the egoist must insist that he is justified in both his beliefs and his actions and that no further explanation or reasons other than those provided by (i) are necessary. Thus, no matter what *K* does, that action will be out of harmony with one of his (moral) beliefs. If he does not take steps to prevent *B* from assassinating him, his act of omission will be clearly contrary to his (correct) beliefs that he ought to become president, and that he ought to prevent *B* from assassinating him. If *K* does take these steps, his act will be contrary to his (correct) belief that *B* is doing what *B* (morally) ought to do, what *B* is morally justified in doing.

One of the many situations in which we engage in "moral argument" with others is that in which we hope to convince our interlocutor that we are justified in doing what we have proposed doing, *thereby* removing their opposition—both physical and verbal—to our so behaving. The teenage daughter tries to convince her father that it is right and proper for sixteen year old girls to date evenings because, if he does agree, then he has no excuse for still withholding his permission (other things being equal). Having agreed, the father is acting at least unreasonably if not irrationally, and in any case, unjustifiably if he does not allow her to date. Normally when we convince someone of the justness of our behavior he comes onto our side, at least reluctantly. Not so in the case of ethical egoism. Under (i) this feature of moral discourse drops out. In Baier's example there is no possibility of K either changing his belief about B's action or changing his own course of action; (i) provides K with no further reasons by which to remove this inconsistency between belief (that B ought to assassinate K) and action (K's prevention of his justified assassination by B). K is in the same position as the father of the teenager. The practical contradiction in question also takes the form of believing both that B ought to do b and that it is not the case that b ought to be done (since K also claims that his action, a, is justified).

As should be clear, this argument, just as Baier's, depends on some version of (v). In connection with this example, this additional premiss could also be expressed as follows:

> (v″) If a certain agent, A, ought to do a certain act, c, then it follows that that act ought to be done and that, at the least, no other agent can be justified in preventing that act from being done.

To show that moral assessment is possible on (i) and that the charge of practical contradiction is not relevant, the egoist must argue against (v). This can be done in the following way: There are areas of rule-governed activity in which neither (v) nor the notion of practical contradiction apply in the relevant ways, yet which are otherwise similar—e.g., competitive games. To escape the above criticisms, the ethical egoist must claim that moral activity is (or at least can be without inconsistency) formally similar to competitive-game activity. An actual moral illustration of this similarity is the following (given by Broad—in time of actual war—while characterizing common sense views concerning our obligations):

> It is held that an Englishman, as such, is under an urgent obligation in certain circumstances to sacrifice his happiness, his development, and his life for England, and is under no such obligation to Germany; and that a German is under an obligation in similar circumstances to make a

similar sacrifice for Germany, and is under no such obligation to England. And so on. It should be noticed that Germans, as well as Englishmen, admit that Englishmen have this peculiar obligation towards England; and that Englishmen, as well as Germans, admit that Germans have this peculiar obligation towards Germany. This is clearly recognized by the saner citizens of both countries even when they are at war with each other.

It seems to me that the fact that an Englishman considers that a German should sacrifice himself for Germany, even when his doing so is detrimental to England, and that a German considers that an Englishman should sacrifice himself for England, even when his doing so is detrimental to Germany, is of some theoretical importance.[10]

Thus, to meet the objection of practical contradiction and to show (v) to be false, the egoist must take seriously the metaphor that life is a game and we are its players. If he is willing to do this, and if it is legitimate to do so, as I think it is, then egoism—as expressed by (i)—appears to be a possible moral theory. For the egoist's purposes, his best example is a competitive game; I shall choose football. Games are paradigms of rule-governed behavior, as every philosopher knows. The rules determine what is required, permitted, and forbidden of the players according to their assigned roles. The rules, conjoined with principles of efficiency, provide the standards of assessment and criticism and are the basis for all quasi-moral (i.e., not merely aesthetic) valuations of play and players. Little in detail need be said to see the appropriateness of this model. There is a point to games, a value or values which they promote. And importantly, this point cannot be that team A wins (comes out on top), or that team B wins (comes out on top), since only one team will win and spectators will do neither. Rather, it is the activity itself which is the point (one can play a good game and lose). And in order for there to be any activity at all there has to be a conflict, and therefore opposing teams A and B. A's goal (i.e., self-interest) is to win, that is, to score more points than B; similarly for B. In any given situation what A should (ought to) do is determined by A's goal in the game, namely, to win; and whatever this is, it will be contrary to B's goal and B ought to prevent A's doing it. Thus in any particular situation it will be right that A do y and also right that B prevent A's doing y. In directing their actions this way each team will be doing what they ought. It would be strange to object that team A, for example, was practically inconsistent. This is the way things should be in football (as in war); indeed, it is a point of censure that a team is not "really" trying (in some sports—e.g., boxing and some styles of

---

[10] Broad, *op. cit.*, pp. 53–54.

wrestling—participants can be penalized for deficient effort). Similarly, the egoist maintains that this is the way the good life is to be realized. Just as the rule "x ought to do y iff y is in x's self-interest" works without difficulty in football where "self-interest" is winning the game, it will work without difficulty in life. Decision situations for egoism and decision situations for football are parallel because: (1) they are both conflict situations, (2) they are both practical situations in that answers to "what should (must) x do?" must be given and can be justified and criticized, and (3) in both cases what will count as reasons for and justifications of a certain course of action will be determined by the nature (ends) of the activity and the roles of the participants. If competitive games are respectable rule-governed activity, then so is egoistic behavior as determined by, for example, rule (i). The differences between the two are minor and not to this point.

V

In the preceding discussion, I have given reasons for thinking that ethical egoism as expressed by (i) is a possible moral principle. I have given a negative defense, for in particular, I have tried to show how ethical egoism can meet the following serious charges: (A) that it does not provide a decision procedure and hence, because it cannot guide an agent, that it cannot be a moral principle, (B) that though it can guide behavior, it cannot be used by the critic to assess morally someone else's behavior, and (C) that though it can guide behavior, it can do so only at the expense of making the agent's actions contradict his beliefs. These, in addition to universality, are all necessary conditions of a moral principle and are all satisfied by (i). Thus there are no formal grounds for excluding (i); conduct may clearly be determined and justified according to it, and such conduct in each particular case would clearly be egoistic conduct.

What else can the opponent say in argument against the egoist? The following remarks which I shall give in Sect. VI are suggested to me by Kant (though here I wish to make no claims of exegetical correctness); I shall examine the egoist's defense in Sect. VII.

VI

An egoist is, above all, a person who takes the satisfaction of his own self-interest to be the ultimate value; this is the goal and end of his actions. However, in accepting ethical egoism, i.e., in universalizing his own mode of behavior, he must to some degree give up the ultimateness of his own self-interest, for (i) makes each person's self-interest of equal value and insofar as one agrees to (i) one must agree to the equality. In a world in which people's interests totally or largely coincide or are complementary this feature of (i) will have only a negligible effect upon his egoism. But in a world in which there are serious conflicts of interest and a shortage of many desirable goods, a sharp contrast between what might be called individual egoism and ethical egoism emerges. In such a world it would be against the egoist's interest for all to pursue seriously their own self-interest and therefore against his interest that everyone *ought* to do as (i) says. Hence he cannot adopt (i) without to some degree denying or giving up his own self-interest; the two are not completely compatible.

Thus, it has been frequently pointed out that, if the egoist's purpose is to secure his own self-interest, in a world of conflict it would be against that self-interest to advocate (i), i.e., to inform others of their moral duties. It has also been pointed out that in such a situation the egoist has the best of reasons—moral reasons—to refrain from advocation, for he ought not to act against his interest. The egoist would, therefore, on his own principle have to hold that principle silently. The problem here is more serious than suspected, for in addition to advocation, the egoist must—for moral reasons—refrain from engaging, at least from seriously engaging, in a wide variety of behavior typical of morality. He will not be able to enter into moral discussions, for to debate a moral issue will ultimately require him to express and argue for (i). This will not be to his interest for at least the reason that others will become suspicious of him and cease to trust him. He will not be able to advise others as to what they ought to do. If it is objected that he can advise them as long as their interests do not conflict, it will be sufficient to remark that it is not to his interest to have his moral views known. To do so is to make pertinent a request for reasons and for a justification of his views; again he would be required to expose his moral beliefs—to his detriment since it would, so to speak, aid and comfort the enemy. Finally, he cannot even teach (i) to his children for that, among other things, could surely give them a reason for abandoning him in his old age.

He can, of course, lie in such situations. Thus when B comes to E for advice and B's interest conflicts with E's, E can tell B that he should do x which in reality is in E's interest but not in B's. Again, this only goes to make the point; E is not sincerely advising B, he is pretending to do so (pretending *sincerely* to advise him; he is, of course, advising him) and so really deceiving and manipulating him. E knows perfectly well (as an ethical egoist) what B ought to do.

Finally, part of the point of appealing to a moral principle to justify behavior is to convince others that their (sometimes forcible) opposition to this behavior is unwarranted and ought to be withdrawn. This point is doomed to frustration for two reasons: (1) justifying one's behavior in terms of (i) gives an opponent no reason to cease his opposition if maintaining it would be in his interest, and (2) it will not be to the egoist's interest to justify publicly his behavior to others and thereby run the risk of converting them to egoism.

It is paradoxical to maintain on the one hand that one believes and has adopted a certain moral principle, namely, to the effect that *everyone ought* to act in a certain way, that is, that a certain state of affairs ought to exist (everyone's *pursuing* his self-interest though not necessarily achieving it), which is to claim, surely, that everyone's so behaving is desirable, and yet on the other hand be committed by that same principle to actions which are in effect denials of that principle, denials that such a state of affairs either ought to exist or is desirable. It would seem that morality under (i) would have lost its purpose—at least insofar as this purpose is embodied and reflected in these moral activities as outlined above—i.e., advocation, defense and justification, moral instruction, etc.; this is very strange and it seems peculiar in these circumstances to any longer speak of (i) as a *moral* principle and hence of the egoist as being morally justified in behaving as he does.

Thus, granted the "formal" soundness of (i) as shown by the previous discussion, and hence in that respect its possibility as a moral principle, a question can still be raised; namely, is it an expression of *egoism* as it claims to be. Some reason has been given to doubt that it is, namely, that an egoist should find it undesirable that everyone behave as *he* does and hence on the grounds of his own egoism should not agree to (adopt) the principle that everybody ought to so behave. And in the sense that no egoist would adopt (i) (given certain not implausible assumptions), (i) is not an expression of egoism (this, I think, would be one way of putting the Kantian criticism of ethical egoism). This has been a major source of objection against ethical egoism; the charge now becomes: granted (i) is a possible moral principle in one sense, it is inadequate as an expression of egoism, and must therefore be an expression of something somewhat different. If one cannot adopt ethical egoism from egoistic interests, then it seems that anyone holding (i) must have modified or given up their egoism to some degree; one could adopt it from utilitarian interests, but only in a world where interests were generally in harmony, and then one would only instrumentally be an egoist and really a utilitarian. For (i) to be an expression of egoism an egoist, at least a "disinterested" egoist, must be able to hold it. That any holder of (i) must be "disinterested" is to be expected, for by adopting a view that everybody ought to behave in a certain way, one is taking a disinterested position. And above, doubt has been cast on the possibility of actually maintaining such a position of disinterested egoism.

In the conflict situation one is faced with the following dilemma: (1) the more one stresses the "disinterested" and "moral" aspects of adopting a moral principle which seem to require sincere participation in the activities of morality, the more one tends to realize other than egoist values, namely, those realized in competitive game situations—for example: conflict, struggle and competition, strength, craft and strategic ability, excitement, danger and insecurity; here one tends to be an egoist only instrumentally. (2) But the more one stresses the "material" (here egoist) aspects of adopting a moral principle which require applying and following the principle, the more one tends to shut out the disinterested and moral aspects essential to being an *ethical* egoist. This dilemma makes the ethical egoist a funny sort of egoist: he both is and isn't an egoist. Kant would say of such a person that there was a "contradiction in his will," meaning that in adopting (i) the egoist was both seeking his own interest and promoting a state of affairs inimical to that interest. Kant would regard this as a fatal defect; that is, while (i) is clearly a possible principle of conduct, it is not an expression of egoism. And considering of what it is an expression, it is quite unattractive. One may surely use it to guide and assess conduct but in doing so one is tending to be an egoist only instrumentally. For (i) to be a fully satisfactory expression of egoism it would have to be the case that the egoist found the consequences of everyone behaving as prescribed desirable, but in a state where interests conflict this is impossible.

VII

I think that the ethical egoist can meet this type of objection and I think further that his success in doing so has great significance to the "foundations of morality." In this final section I shall give only a sketch of the egoist's reply and its importance to at least certain meta-ethical positions.

I wish to begin by distinguishing between two essentially different conceptions of morality. They may be crudely differentiated in terms of the basic question they each ask (or rather which the moral agent is to ask):

(1) What should *I* do?
(2) What should *we* do?

In each case it is a single person asking the question; and in each case universalization is requisite insofar as there is a claim to reasonableness and justification, i.e., insofar as an *answer* for a question is being sought. But the value systems which justify such answers may differ importantly according to which question is asked.

This distinction is, I think, based upon and more properly explained in terms of two conceptions of intrinsic value which I shall term (1) the formal, and (2) the material (cf. Kant) or objective. In case (2) the notion of intrinsic value is that of an objective value common to all (of value to everyone); hence everyone has an obligation to promote it. Utilitarianism—the greatest happiness principle—and "supremacy of the state" views are good examples of this conception. An example in a different way is Kurt Baier and the "good reasons" approach. I call these views the "material" conception of intrinsic value because they hold either that there is something (e.g., [consciousness of] pleasure and knowledge—Ross) which is of value to everyone equally, or else hold a view concerning the justification of actions which requires either that the interests of each be taken equally into account and/or that some notion of "common interest" be employed.

In case (1) the notion of intrinsic value is that of final or ultimate value, where the value is ultimate only in the sense that for that particular person it is the basis of his other values. Aristotle suggests this conception of intrinsic value at various points and I think that it is the one most in harmony with his system.[11] It conceives intrinsic value as relative to the individual. I characterize this view as the "formal" conception of intrinsic value for the following reasons: It may be quite possible to give a formal characterization of intrinsic value—either in generic terms, e.g., happiness and self-interest, or in terms of principles of justification, e.g., as Hare or Brandt do

[11] I have in mind particularly Aristotle's conception of the proper function (-ing) of an organism, defined in terms of the ends it naturally pursues (cf. especially I, 7 of the *Ethics*). Note also his comments on the relativity of the mean to the agent and the situation (cf. II, 6).

(commitment, qualified attitude)—such that its material content (i.e., what is actually intrinsically valuable) will vary from individual to individual, even conflict among individuals, and will depend on varying empirical matters. Thus on Aristotle's view it is clearly quite possible that my actual good (end; intrinsic value) might seriously conflict with your actual good, though generically they are both the same. It is part of view (1) that whenever such a conflict as this occurs there are no further moral questions to raise. What is intrinsically valuable for one is not for another; this is perfectly consistent. Both are justified and are so in virtue of appealing to the same principles of justification which determine content ("matter") only in conjunction with empirical data and which might determine conflicting contents.

The objections to ethical egoism given in Sect. I, if successful, would work against egoism on either view (1) or (2), though they have been couched usually in terms appropriate to view (2) in an attempt to make the strongest case (cf. especially (A) and (C)). Even in view (2) they are unsuccessful. The objection in (VI) assumes view (2) and is successful in virtue of this fact. Thus, one way of meeting his critic is to retreat from view (2) to view (1), which, I suggest, upon examination the ethical egoist will find to be quite comfortable and what he had in mind all along.

But before examining this "retreat" in more detail, it is interesting to note that the egoist could remain with view (2) without too disastrous consequences. Even on view (2), since the objections given in Sect. I fail, it is still possible to ask "What are we to do?" and receive as an answer "Each pursue his own self-interest." (i) could follow from utilitarian considerations, as has already been mentioned. But the egoist could also revise his stance slightly and consider of intrinsic value, in the material sense, the following: "each man's pursuing his self-interest alone." Or as Eliot says in another connection: "But perhaps neither gain nor loss. For us there is only the trying. The rest is not our business."[12]

Is this no longer egoism? In one sense *no*—namely, in the sense that

---

[12] T. S. Eliot, *The Four Quartets*, "East Coker," V, in *The Complete Poems and Plays: 1909–1950* (New York, 1962), p. 128.

Or perhaps Heracleitus: "Homer was wrong in saying: 'Would that strife might perish from among Gods and men!' He did not see that he was praying for the destruction of the universe; for, if his prayer were heard, all things would pass away" (No. 44). "We must know that war is common to all and strife is justice, and that all things come into being and pass away through strife" (No. 62). "Men do not know how how what is at variance agrees with itself. It is an attunement of opposite tensions, like that of the bow and lyre" (No. 45). Fragments translated by John Burnett in *Early Greek Philosophy* (New York, 1957), pp. 136–137.

the egoist is one who claims that it is his own interest alone that is important. Thus, Kant is right: egoism, where self-interest is the value, cannot be willed to be universal where the cash value of "willed-to-be" is participation in certain characteristic public activities (cf. VI). But our revised egoist can participate without inconsistency in these public activities. Here the game metaphor becomes instructive. Participation in such public activities is analogous to making the rules and nature of the game clear to the participants, a necessary condition of having a good game ("Now go out and fight a good, clean fight"); following the moral rules is analogous to playing the game.

While it is true that strictly speaking egoism has become an instrumental value, even as such it can retain its egoistic "flavor." This is evident when it is applied in situations of irreconcilable conflict along lines mentioned earlier. It is doubtful that a utilitarian justification of (i) could succeed in such a situation. It is perhaps difficult to imagine having the outlook needed in order to advocate (i) in such an inhospitable state of affairs; nonetheless, it seems a possibility, and perhaps the professional soldier or the principal of *Zorba the Greek* are approximations.

The important point is that the argument in (VI) works only for this "material" conception of morality and intrinsic value, and not for what I have called the "formal" conception. That this is so can be quickly seen. The argument depends upon a conception of morality defined, at least in part, by the public activities of advocating and prescribing, justifying, and defending moral views. Because these activities necessarily involve other agents and because they have as a purpose agreement in ends (cf. Baier on the resolution of conflict as the essence of morality), they must presuppose view (2). On view (1) none of these activities is necessary nor is there a common end in question; the agent's only concern is to discover what *he* ought to do and, as I have argued above, this need not require any reference to others. The only justification the ethical egoist need engage in on this view is justification to himself, and in doing this he need consider only his own interests as of value. To others it may be best to lie, to agree with them, to try to convince them of utilitarianism, or perhaps just to look embarrassed; such behavior is unproblematic on view (1). Thus I conclude that ethical egoism is certainly a possible moral view and that any refutation of it will require extensive argumentation involving features at the very heart of ethics.

University of California, Berkeley

III

Moral Nihilism

G. P. HENDERSON

I WANT to examine what has been called moral nihilism—not so much in order to identify examples of it in the community, as to ask whether it can be coherent or not (without prejudice to its existence, so to speak; for incoherent attitudes can exist). The question "Is morality something that one can opt out of?" is rather in the air at the moment. Some people try to answer it by maintaining that "Morality is something you are born into," and this statement as it stands is certainly obscure enough to merit philosophical discussion. I shall concentrate on the notion of "opting out" of morality, or, as I shall say for convenience of diction, "renouncing" morality. What would it be to renounce morality? Let us take it that the renunciation involves (in some way yet to be determined) all of the various moral dimensions, *good-bad, right-wrong, obligatory-forbidden*, and whatever others are recognized, and thus whatever specific kinds of goodness, rightness, obligation, etc., they comprehend.

I propose to look at the matter in terms first of realist and secondly of non-realist theories of goodness, rightness, obligatoriness and so on. (The discussion of non-realist theories will be the longer.) Suppose, then, a realist context: the words "goodness," "rightness," and "obligatoriness" are to be taken as naming qualities, of dispositions, acts, relationships, and so on; real qualities to be discerned, and not depending for their existence or character on the discernment. Our ideas of them could be either innate or adventitious. The point would be that the qualities were there to be taken account of, and, furthermore, they would be there whether we adopted them as objects of pursuit or not. They would be features of the environment we are born into. We could not but believe in them, whatever policy we adopted with regard to them. So, let us suppose, we recognize good but have nothing to do with it; we allow that a certain course of action is right but dissociate ourselves from it. We agree that such-and-such an arrangement is just, but we will have no part in it. In each of these instances we must add "as such." The nihilist (if we may now so name whoever it is that sets himself to renounce moral dimensions in the ways indicated) is not supposed to be lapsing into inaction, or even to be refraining from action which we should normally treat as being morally qualified. No, but it is to be a contingent matter whether what he does is good, right, just or not, the point being that he never does it *as* one or another of these things.

It seems necessary, though, to take the possibility of systematic hypocrisy into account here. I said that it was a contingent matter whether what a nihilist does is good (etc.) or not. How this is so varies according to whether he is prepared to be hypocritical or not. What he renounces is moral assent, not necessarily moral conformity. For he would still conform if he regarded the "moral" qualities simply as factors in the calculation of what is in his interest, opponent's pieces in the game of life, which as played by him is a particularly deep one. He would be playing it with knowledge, but without virtue; doing the good, the right thing, not because it was good or right (although he would realize *that* it was), but because others thought it so. This sort of conformism could be systematic and sophisticated; habit might become part of it, but could never be allowed to take it over if it were to remain calculating. The appropriate maxim would be: "Act in allegiance to what is moral if it is in your interest so to do." There is no obvious incoherence in this, even on a realist theory: any more than in the maxim "Act in allegiance to Smith's regime if it is in your interest so to do."

A less calculating conformism is, of course, possible. It may indeed actually be found in the mild nihilism of the emotionally uncommitted: of those who don't get excited about morality, or moral issues, but who suppose that there would be no point, no real advantage, in not, for the most part, behaving morally.

So much for the hypocritical type of nihilism, in the present context. The conformists just described represent one type for whom it would be a contingent matter whether what they did was good, right, just, or not. But there is a second possible type, and this type I find rather harder to describe. Let me try, however, to describe, against a realist background, what might be called conscientious nihilism (if the word "conscientious" can be taken here as having a merely descriptive import). The conscientious nihilist would be a person who recognized that there exist moral qualities but who refused to take them into account. Unlike the conformist he would even disregard them as a factor in other people's attitudes. He would act as if they were not there. Would this be a coherent way of proceeding?

It would be coherent, I suppose, to the same extent that it would remain coherent for someone to refuse to take into account the fact that things are colored. He would have to perform some pretty difficult feats of abstraction, but in no circumstances would the fact that things are colored make any difference to what *he* did with regard to them. It would be a hit-or-miss matter whether the color nihilist did the same sort of things with, say, a scarlet tulip as the committed colorist did: and similarly with the moral nihilist's actions about what is moral in one way or another.

One might suppose that even in a realist world it would be *possible* to act in the restricted way thus indicated, but it is another question whether the policy of doing so would have any point. Can any point be stated coherently? One could make out a case for refusing to take "moral" qualities into account only if one held that the recognition of these qualities was an irrelevance, that it made no difference to anything that anyone did, that the qualities were of a merely secondary kind. It would make no difference in that one could take just as profitable or sagacious an account of other people's doings if one left their "moral" motives out of account as if one took them into account: for what they did in the name of goodness (etc.) would really be done in terms of something else altogether. But this case would be indefensible because it is self-contradictory. It would be to hold that the alleged qualities were *un*real in the sense that, so far as the acts, dispositions, or relationships possessing them were concerned, they were completely reducible to others. And this would be to deny them ontological status *per se*, in a way somewhat similar to that in which Russell denied meaning *per se* to denoting expressions. Thus it would be inconsistent with the realist metaphysic being presupposed.

Granted, though, that conscientious nihilism is incoherent in the way just suggested, isn't also, in the end, what I have been calling conformist or hypocritical nihilism? It might be suggested that the latter policy is just putting off the evil day, as it were, of coming to terms with conscientious nihilism. We could, *any* of us, become alive to other people's conformism, and in that event, the conformism would cease to have its own special point. (The gaff would be blown on it.) This, I think, must be admitted, but it remains true that short of such discovery, a degree of hypocritical conformity would have its point. The conformist does differ from the conscientious nihilist in his metaphysic. He allows that moral qualities do make a difference to people's actions in that many actions aren't the same as what they would be in the absence of such qualities: so that what is done in the name of goodness (etc.) can't be treated as if it weren't so done, provided that prudence comes into the reckoning at all.

May we now look at the whole topic in another setting, without presupposing a realist view of moral "qualities"? Suppose now that our moral concepts are factitious, that they are, in a manner, social constructions. (I do not intend this supposition, taken by itself, to imply that moral concepts are any less important than we normally think they are.) "Society" could then be seen as consisting of three classes: (i) those who adopt and assent to certain more or less generally recognized "moral" prescriptions or norms, (ii) those who conform, without assent, to such prescriptions, and (iii) those who neither assent nor conform. Like their opposite numbers discussed under the realist heading but in rather different ways, (ii) and (iii) would be held to have renounced morality. We can now have a fresh look at what this would be.

On the face of it, moral nihilism is an easier, more natural position to hold when it is not described against a realist background. For example, a nihilist might claim to be "refusing to accept arbitrarily-imposed social standards." But this would be rather a windy way of putting his claim. There is nothing arbitrary about the general treatment of some things (for present purposes it does not matter what) as good, others as bad, of some courses of action as right, others as wrong. We are talking about the habitude of moral categorization, which may fairly be thought of as a natural, indeed necessary feature (in the dialectical sense) of the development of society. The nihilist, then, needs to be less dramatic. So let him just claim to be making a break with a certain established general way of evaluating people, their dispositions, their actions and so on, and consequently with any sort of prescriptive principles which depend on that sort of evaluation.

Under the realist heading the conscientious nihilist was criticized for being less aware than the conformist of the implications of realism for the conduct of life. If there are "real" moral qualities it is natural to argue that moral attitudes must be irreducibly distinctive ones and that it is pointless to behave as if they aren't. But if the language of moral "qualities" is systematically misleading, then by refusing to speak it, one will at least not be comporting oneself as if the world were a poorer thing, ontologically, than it is. Certainly the world is different for having the language of moral qualities, but it is not obvious that the conformist now has the advantage over the conscientious nihilist of not ignoring what is, so to speak, built in with the bricks. What I propose to do, therefore, is to advert to the conformist only incidentally: it is the nihilist of integrity who now interests me most, under the present heading.

So, we are to think of the nihilist in the following terms: he recognizes that there exist moral ways of thinking, recognizes no necessity to subscribe to them and, for himself, renounces or foreswears them. On what grounds could he defend his position?

His grounds could be that moral ways of thought are only apparently different from certain others, for example, economic: they can always be translated into those others, which there is some reason to prefer. It would follow from this view that the existence of distinctively "moral" motives is an illusion.

If this view is correct, however, what is the point of renouncing morality? If moral ways of thinking amount to nothing different from what certain others do, what does it matter which set of terms we prefer? There must be profit in abandoning the moral ones and this can be the case only if these are in some way misleading, if they do say something distinctive, but in some undesirable (that is, disadvantageous) way.

The nihilist's stand would thus seem to be on some pernicious or otherwise objectionable difference between moral ways of thought and others, such as that the former misrepresent truth or that they are over-demanding: the grounds might vary so much. At any rate there would be a difference which he sees some point in setting himself against. How are we to indicate it?

One possible line of approach (amongst others, no doubt) is as follows: Moral categorization corresponds to nothing in the nature of things but just expresses a set of habits of commending and prescribing, distinctive of a class or group with which one is under no necessity to identify oneself. The class or group may even have become outmoded, a fact which may be disguised by the inertia of language-habit.[1] Even supposing that the class or group has not become outmoded, there still might be some point in not identifying oneself with it. For example: It might just be that one hasn't the energy to be moral and that one decides to give up trying. This would be a relatively irrational decision in that it took no account of long-term interest. All it could rest on would be the idea that any morally-motivated action involved more effort than we felt like making. (For that matter, a realist version of the same attitude seems conceivable.) Anyhow, whether misguidedly or not one can say: "I renounce morality: it just isn't worth the effort. I prefer my own

---

[1] I remark parenthetically that we can of course identify ourselves with such habits calculatingly, that is, go through the motions of commending and prescribing in the approved manner, with disguised cynicism. But let us get back to "renouncing."

immediate ease." This need not be said prescriptively—a point which may turn out to be of importance later. Alternatively, and more rationally (it would seem), one could come to a decision that morality as such was mistaken policy, that the general aims, advantages, or benefits (construed non-morally, of course) to which one's progress through life was directed were simply not served by it: hence one could acknowledge its existence (and, if one were a cynic, trade in terms of it), but one would not be moved by it. More positively, one might specify one's objective as being self-realization, perhaps, or self-fulfillment or freedom of a special sort—and if asked for what reason one wanted to be free, might reply "For no reason. I just prefer being free, exactly as I prefer marmalade to jam."

With regard to each of these statements of aim one wants to ask: Is there any general impossibility, in the sense of logical incoherence, about it or not? It seems perfectly natural to say that in each case a policy is being adopted: in the first, a policy of imperturbable action, and in the second a policy of (if we may so put it) rational economic action. Is there any reason why, as some have supposed, we have to call these policies themselves "moral," and hence to let moral considerations in again through a first-floor window? I stress again the lack of difference between them. For the present purposes the second differs from the first only in being less lazy. Are they, then, "moral" or not?

It is worth reflecting a little, to begin with, on the use of the word "policy" in this context. If it implies that morality is one policy amongst others, that nihilism and morality are alternatives on the same footing, then its use may be open to question. For it would settle the issue against those who would hold that merely *qua* policy, nihilism is subject to moral criticism. If nihilism and morality are alternatives on the same footing, then they may be compared as wise or foolish, sagacious or muddle-headed, prudent or imprudent, profitable or not, but they cannot be compared in terms of moral goodness or badness or any other moral terms, because, *ex hypothesi*, neither is subordinate to the other in a classificatory or predicative way. So that if anyone wants to show that nihilism *qua* policy is, even in a limiting sense, "moral," in other words that it is incoherent, he must not imply that morality itself is a policy. Instead, morality must be represented as some sort of general framework of action, or as a set of criteria necessarily relevant to any policy, or as a touchstone to which any policy must be brought. And this would be tantamount to showing that a contradiction lies in the declaration, "I renounce morality," where the word "renounce" is allowed to be a policy-expressive term: in short, there could be no such policy as the renunciation of morality, at any rate if a minimum condition of anything's being a policy is its coherence. Such is the thesis which those who hold moral nihilism to be a crypto-moral attitude are required to prove. What are the prospects of proving it?

Some people find the renunciation of morality beyond their power to imagine. "What you are renouncing isn't morality," they are inclined to say, "it's only a way or a degree of being moral." "Honor among thieves" is their slogan. Even amongst the sliest and the toughest characters you will always find something analogous to honor among thieves if you look hard enough. But can't I just renounce even this limited honesty or its counterpart? Name *any* virtue and I'm prepared to renounce it in its turn. However long I go on doing this, or however confidently I claim the right to go on, can you imagine that at some stage I must be stoppable? Can you insist, that is, that in some way which eludes this policy of *seriatim* renunciation my thinking remains articulated by "moral" values, moral goodness in some manner, rightness after some fashion, or perhaps even just some vague kind of moral importance?

A favorite reply to this question is that I adhere to certain values, moral values, in spite of myself. My "renunciation" is only verbal. It might be said, for example, that I am really valuing independence, freedom from any sort of social constraint at all: I am setting a value on a certain mode of life, which I am treating, indeed, as a good in itself and which I act as if I had the right to maintain. ("Good" and "right" don't need to have a place in *my* vocabulary for this to be so.) Or it might be replied that I am committed to certain second-order, if not first-order values—the value of a way of life which must be distinguished as such by the presence or absence of this, that, or the next first-order value. Or again it might be suggested that some values are ambiguous in status. *Freedom*, for example, might represent one moral value amongst others, but it might also be a dominant, colligating value, like *justice* in the *Republic*. Conceivably one might renounce it in the first sense but not in the second. At any rate an analogue of it might be retained in the wider context—like Plato's tyrannical freedom which is consistent with all sorts of bondage when it comes to the bit.

The way of life which is talked about in these replies to moral nihilism obviously needs some further description. It is perhaps worth stressing that a moral nihilist needn't be all that conspicuous, or so improbable a character as to cock a snook at society and at individuals in every way and at every moment. For one can renounce morality and remain within the law. One's policy can be prudential to that extent at least. This being allowed, how could a nihilist's way of life be described, in general terms? One well-known but not yet too well-worn answer is that it consists in treating other people as means, not as ends. The answer implies that their treatment as ends, whatever that involves, actually constitutes morality: so that consideration for other people, whatever it amounts to, is not just a conventional moral virtue amongst others, but is the basis of all morality. (It involves not interfering with other people's personalities, out of a certain respect for them rather than because you enjoy them, for then they may be part of *your* enjoyment.) A nihilist therefore cuts out considerateness, much as if he were getting rid of a useless appendix. He does so as a matter of policy, on principle: to secure his own benefit in *some* sense, his desiderata or what he takes to be such: on principle, keeping himself right, because he has once thought the matter out and, either as a result of more or less conclusive deliberation or to save himself trouble, has decided to treat people, without exception, in a non-considerate fashion. His decision has its rationale. Is it, all the same, coherent?

I take this to be once again the problem posed by Thrasymachus and Callicles; and the policy described, if it is allowed to stand in the terms suggested, may more readily appear unprofitable than incoherent. But these terms might be disputed. Someone might dispute the idea that the treatment of other people as ends constitutes morality or even is essential to morality. The proof might be the logical possibility of a wild metaphysical egoism ("I am God," or "I am God's anointed") according to which one is oneself the point, the *raison d'être* or the τέλος of the universe, so that it would follow *a fortiori* that the universe was morally geared to oneself. ("It is good and right and proper that the world should serve *me*.") However, the alleged moral consequence does not ring true. The attitude described is in effect a solipsism ("other people don't *exist* as I do"), and it is difficult to see that moral values can be accommodated by it. To suggest that I alone am admirable is to put admiration out of place. There is nothing to assess me against, no scope for a *scale* of values. I am just unique. The metaphysics of egoism may therefore be possible, but its claim to have accomplished the rape of morality seems unconvincing.

I may be wrong about this, though. In any case one wants to ask whether there isn't any less crazy setting in which morality can be thought of *minus* the treatment of other people as ends, thus leaving

D

it possible for the so-called "nihilist" to be convicted of having, even in a limiting sense of the term, a "morality."

All I can do here is to say that I don't think there is and that the logical incoherence of nihilism remains to me unproved. I take morality to be a system of restraints and initiatives the rationale of which is just the recognition that I am not alone, and that what I am not alone with is a collection of other me's: the recognition of this plus an assent to it in the sense of a sort of self-identification with others involving, so far as I am concerned, the possibility of their self-expression, their self-development too (the possibility resting either in my not preventing these things or in my positively encouraging them). It is not surprising that from time to time in moral philosophy altruism has been presented as a function of sympathy. For in so much of what we do to help others no calculation is involved. Others have interests, and it may or may not be in my interest that they should in general be assisted to cultivate theirs: but to me normally, this is a consequential, theoretical question. I assist them because I feel with them. As an alternative to basing morality on sympathy one might argue the consideration that, other people being other me's, it is best (most productive of happiness) for each that all should be satisfied in various ways, and that the ways should be taken cooperatively. The result would be a rational morality and not one of sentiment. But if, in the attempt to reason out its basis, I were to disover that altruism was, apparently, seriously against my interests, then I should be landed with Plato's problem over again. If one still wanted to defend altruism, one would have to take the line that egoism, in spite of apparent successes, was self-defeating, that it was destructive of a human being as such to abandon altruism (or, renounce morality if this means the same thing). That, apparently, was Plato's own position. The sort of incoherence to which he tried to reduce his "unjust" man, however, was not of the type which I have been discussing in connection with attacks on moral nihilism. Plato's argument was directed towards the ultimate pointlessness of the unjust man's existence: and it would be not untypical of argument between philosophical altruism and philosophical egoism to have resort to such terms in the end. But whatever incoherence these indicate, it does not consist in ascribing to the unjust man a moral position; a moral commitment that will cling to him, do what he may.

What do these considerations add up to? They seem to me to indicate that, except for the physical restraints imposed by law or by other means, or considerations of expediency connected with those, one could conceivably deal with other people in ways totally free. One could well talk a language which contained no moral vocabulary. What a nihilistic policy values, what it prefers, doesn't come under moral categories, even second-order categories. These, like first order, would be appropriate only within a committed other-person ontology.

There remains one avenue to be explored. In a symposium held some years ago, Mr. N. L. Cooper argued that moral nihilism was in fact the limiting case of a morality and that the nihilist *can* be said to make a moral judgment.[2] The nihilist's slogan is that nothing matters morally. He rejects the concept of moral importance in all dimensions, those of *good–bad, ought–ought not* and any others that might be recognized. This rejection consists in asserting that the concept has no application. But anyone who does this, according to Cooper, will "use the concept, and in using the moral concept we necessarily make a moral judgment"; so that in general the concept of moral importance is one which we cannot avoid using, if only to reject it.

I am afraid it is not clear to me that the moral nihilist does take up a moral attitude (i.e., make a moral judgment) by rejecting the concept of moral importance. In the first instance it is a "logical" or semantical attitude that he adopts. To assert of *any* concept that it has no application is to do no more, immediately, than commit oneself to a semantical rule. The nihilist would be taking up a moral attitude only if he said that the concept *ought to have* no application, or recommended *for certain reasons* (i.e., reasons it would be absurd to say weren't moral ones) that it should have no application. Which could he be expected to do? The second alternative either is self-contradictory or involves him in an unending regress of moral languages. He would obviously wish to avoid this. So he must insist on saying that the concept has or is to have no application. But, we are entitled to ask, for whom? *We* do obviously apply it, and in a perfectly sensible way, since it makes a great difference what we call morally important and what we don't. It must be for him alone. He may be forced to recognize other people's use of the concept, but he refuses to adopt it for himself. He does not, therefore, "use" it. The sort of thing he proposes to say is not that some action *x* is morally indifferent, but that it is indifferent (not that it has no degree of moral importance, but that it has nothing to be called "moral importance"); not that *y* is morally permissible but that it is

---

[2] "Rules and Morality" in *Proceedings of the Aristotelian Society*, Supplementary Volume 33 (1959), see especially pp. 168–172. I am much indebted to Mr. Cooper for helpful criticism of the present essay.

permissible (having nothing such that the question of either imposing it as a duty or forbidding it need even arise). If this is how he speaks, then he is surely not, in the process, making a moral judgment.

But, it might be replied, he is committing himself to the view that morality is unimportant, or, alternatively, that egoism is all-important. And this is his ultimate *moral* commitment, because it displays what he regards as of *supreme* importance, as having priority over all else.[3]

It does display this, one may agree. But are we forced on this account to call the man's ultimate assessment of importance "moral"? There are various ways of putting the point that we are not. One would be to urge that his judgment is for himself only, that it is neither prescriptive nor universalizable, and is not intended as such. (I anticipated this consideration when I was describing the lazy man who just would not vex himself with morality.) More simply it could be said that neither what ought to be nor what is good (taken in any sense except that of what is desired) comes into his reckoning. That the concept of moral importance has no importance for him *can* be allowed to mean: he does not use it.

In a quite clear sense, then, the moral nihilist refuses to talk other people's language. Is it possible nevertheless to hold that he remains committed to morality in some other way? The answer is—not in any other way that you can bring home to him. Suppose we say that he is truly subject to moral criticism by others: that he really ought to do something about his personal relationships: and that not to adopt morality as the touchstone of policy is immoral. Even on the assumption that what we are saying makes sense, clearly we cannot get home to him along this route. We can, of course, argue that not to adopt morality as a touchstone of policy is disadvantageous. But this would be another matter. What it comes to is that once again we are involved in Plato's worry—how to get at the professed nihilist *except* by persuading him that to have no regard to morality doesn't pay. For it is only a substitute satisfaction that persuasion of this kind provides.

University of Dundee

---

[3] Cf. N. L. Cooper, "Morality and Importance," *Mind*, vol. 77 (1968).

IV

Supererogation and Duties

MICHAEL STOCKER*

IN this paper I shall explore some of the similarities and dissimilarities between acts that fulfill duties and supererogatory acts. Duties, we may say, are right to do and wrong not to do; while supererogatory acts, we may say, are right to do and *not* wrong not to do.[1] Given this clear difference, what question, it might be asked, would provide less insight into the relations among ethical concepts than the one I am proposing to explore? I trust that what I shall say will provide an adequate answer and rebuttal to this charge. For I shall show that it is difficult, in any interesting or illuminating way, to distinguish between acts that fulfill duties and supererogatory acts. Much more has to be said about them than merely: some of them—viz., duties—are right to do and wrong not to do, and the others—viz., supererogatory acts—are right to do and not wrong not to do. I believe that at least some of what I shall say is important not only for understanding these concepts and their interrelations, but also for the enterprise of finding out which ethical concepts are, or can be used as, primitive or basic.

---

* Versions of this essay have been read at a meeting of the University of Chicago philosophy department seminar in February 1966 and at the Western Division meetings of the APA in May 1966. I am happy to take this opportunity to thank all those who have discussed this material with me, and I should especially like to thank Professors William Frankena and Alvin Plantinga for discussions which originally led me to this problem, and Professor Henry West (my commentator at the APA meetings). My thanks are also due to Cornell University for a summer research grant in 1966.

[1] On supererogation see: R. Chisholm, "Supererogation and Offence," *Ratio*, vol. 5 (1963); J. Feinberg, "Supererogation and Rules," *Ethics*, vol. 71 (1960); J. O. Urmson, "Saints and Heroes" in *Essays in Moral Philosophy*, ed. by A. I. Melden (Seattle, Washington, 1958); M. Stocker, *Supererogation*, doctoral dissertation, Harvard, 1966. In this paper I shall not try to distinguish between duties and obligations; nor shall I restrict "duty" to institutional contexts or contexts defined by practices. I take "duty" to be roughly equivalent with "right to do and wrong not to do"—but not that much in this paper really depends on accepting this. My use of "act" does not distinguish between *acts* properly so-called and other *things that are done*. (On this see D. Sachs, "A Few Morals About Acts," *The Philosophical Review*, vol. 75 [1966], especially pp. 91–92.) I trust that my "traditional and philosophical" use of "duty" and "act" will not occasion any difficulty for this paper.

In Sect. I, I shall briefly present some considerations about duty fulfilling acts that will indicate why it is rather difficult to distinguish between such acts and supererogatory acts. In Sect. II, I shall consider and reject an argument to the effect that we should not distinguish between supererogatory acts and duty fulfilling acts since supererogatory acts are really imperfect duty fulfilling acts. In Sect. III, I shall show how to distinguish between supererogatory acts and duty fulfilling acts using *rightness* and *wrongness* as my only moral concepts.

I. DUTIES

We fulfill duties by performing acts—i.e., by performing act tokens, for we cannot perform act types. Nonetheless, it is not a duty to perform any act token. For we could have fulfilled the duty by doing another act token of the appropriate type. For example, even though that returning of the book fulfilled the promise to return the book, many other returnings of the book would have done so as well. Thus it is not true only for imperfect duties that we need do only some—i.e., just any—of the acts open to us to fulfill a duty. This raises two problems here: (i) What is it our duty to do since it is not our duty to do any given act token? (ii) What is the difference between perfect and imperfect duties?

(i) The answer to the first question is that it is simply our duty to exemplify act types. (ii) The answer to the second question is that the only difference between the two sorts of duties is the way acts that fulfill them are individuated. If a duty is perfect, then any duty fulfilling act is considered to be the same. That is, *qua* fulfilling the duty to return the promised book, whether one returns the book with the right hand or the left hand, one is doing the same act: viz., keeping the promise by returning the book. In the case of imperfect duties, however, not every duty fulfilling act is the same. They are individuated by some principle of individuation. In Mill's imperfect duty of beneficence, the principle of individuation is "benefitting a different person or benefitting someone at a different time." That is, for such imperfect duties, duty fulfilling acts are different just in case one person rather than another is benefitted or the benefit is rendered at a different time. (Of course, this is not what Mill said, but it would have been usable by him. It is my reconstruction of his concept to make it clear and consistent.)

Perhaps the following is a better way to bring out the differences between these two sorts of duties. We say that we have a duty (perfect or imperfect) of a certain sort: i.e., to exemplify an act type—say, *returning a book*. We shall represent the type we must exemplify in order to fulfill the duty by 'T'. Imperfect duty fulfilling acts are not considered to be the same just because they are tokens of T; they are individuated by some principle. That principle, or the characteristics in virtue of which it operates, will be represented here by 'U'—and the duty will be said to be imperfect in regard to U. Thus we say:

A has an imperfect duty in respect to U to do act b of type T if and only if act b is a member of the set S of n (possible) acts of type T such as that:

   (i) doing any m ($m>0$) members of S fulfills the duty
   (ii) doing less than m members fails to fulfill the duty
   (iii) n is greater than m ($n>m$)
   (iv) the members of S are individuated relative to U
   (v) b is at most the mth member of S to be done.

Conditions for A's having a perfect duty to do act b of type T are had if conditions (i)–(iii), not–(iv), and (v) obtain.[2]

What is of most importance for this paper is that we see that for both perfect and imperfect duty fulfilling acts, it is possible to do more such acts than are needed to fulfill the duty. This was brought out earlier by noting that it is not one's duty to perform any given act token—even if that act token does fulfill a duty. Rather it is only a duty to exemplify an act type. Thus there are duty fulfilling acts that are *not* wrong not to do. But, therefore, at least some duty fulfilling acts are like supererogatory acts in a very important respect: They are both right to do and *not* wrong not to do.

How then should these importantly different sorts of acts be distinguished from each other? It is to this task that I now turn. I shall make this distinction using *rightness* and *wrongness* as my only moral concepts.

II. Imperfect Duties, Not Supererogatory Acts

Roughly speaking, supererogatory acts are those acts that are right to do and not wrong not to do, and thus not one's duty. I say *roughly speaking* because the doing of supererogatory acts must render the agent praiseworthy. Otherwise, buying oneself an ice cream cone

[2] For a fuller explanation and defense of these claims and definitions see below and my paper "Acts, Perfect Duties, and Imperfect Duties," *The Review of Metaphysics*, vol. 21 (1967).

—right to do and not wrong not to do—would satisfy the above conditions. This is not of great importance here for two reasons: (i) doing imperfect or perfect duty fulfilling acts can render one praiseworthy; (ii) there are acts that are not duties, not supererogatory acts, but are right to do—e.g., buying oneself an ice cream cone. Thus much of what is said in this paper about supererogatory acts also applies to these other acts that are at once right to do, not duties, and not supererogatory.

Supererogation is exemplified not only in the lives and acts of moral saints and heroes, but also in the lives and acts of more ordinary people. I consider all the following acts—or things that are done—to be supererogatory: (i) Going out to dangerous and outlying areas to do medical work, (ii) running into a burning building to save a trapped child, (iii) giving so much to charity that one really feels the pinch, (iv) going out of one's way to see that a stranger in one's town does not get lost, (v) taking a book to a friend to help him complete his research, (vi) buying an ice cream cone, on a hot day, for a child one does not know.

Some, if not most philosophers, have denied the existence of supererogatory acts. Nonetheless such philosophers have, or might have, agreed that the above (and similar) acts are not like other duties even though these acts are duties, too. While agreeing that they are not perfect duties, they could hold that such acts are, or would, fulfill, imperfect duties. Thus they are right to do, not wrong not to do, but not supererogatory.[3]

They could say that while it is not obligatory to do any one of these acts (now considered as types to be exemplified), it is obligatory to do some given number of them. We can represent this claim as follows: Let us use "Dx" for "it is a perfect duty to do act x," and let us designate one of these acts—say, (vi): buying the ice cream cone —by b. Let acts similar to b be acts $c, d, \ldots, k$. The situation is as follows:

$$D\,(b \vee c \vee \ldots \vee k)\ \&\ \sim Db\ \&\ \sim Dc\ \&\ \ldots\ \&\ \sim Dk.$$

If this would account for supererogation, it might well enable philosophers to account for such acts without giving up their neater theories about the relations between value and obligation—and about the nonexistence of supererogatory acts. This account, however, is not sound.

[3] This position is suggested, e.g., by H. Rashdall, *The Theory of Good and Evil* (Oxford, 1907), vol. II, chap. IV, Sect. IV; and by Y. Chopra, "Professor Urmson on 'Saints and Heroes'," *Philosophy*, vol. 38 (1963).

First objection: In saying that an act is, or would fulfill, an imperfect duty, one is saying that it belongs to some set of acts such that it is a duty to do only some—i.e., just any—of these acts. From this it follows that under conceivable circumstances it will be a perfect duty to do any given act or acts from that set. In itself this is neither surprising nor disturbing; for most any act (type) could be a perfect duty—given the appropriate circumstances. What is disturbing, however, is the sort of circumstances that can make any given one of these acts a perfect duty. Such conditions will obtain whenever it is necessary to do that act in order to do the requisite number of acts from that disjoint list. But *that* condition will obtain in rather ordinary and morally uncharged circumstances. Perhaps one simply has not done a sufficient number of such acts in the past, and it is no longer possible to do them. Thus under such ordinary circumstances, any given one of these acts could be one's perfect duty, and thus wrong not to do. But I, for one, am not willing to accept such a possibility—especially for the first acts in my list of six.

This poses a problem for Mill. Consider a man who has not performed sufficient acts of beneficence to discharge that imperfect duty. Now as his end draws near, he has only one chance left to be beneficent. And perhaps there is only one man to whom he can be beneficent. What sort of duty does he have to perform that act of beneficence? And what sort of duty does he have to that man?

Second objection: If a correct representation of imperfect duties was given by that disjunctive list, then once the agent has done the requisite number of acts, it will not be his duty—either perfect or imperfect—to do any of the others. (Here, I leave aside the problem of "over" obligation—on the model of over or multiple causation.) But what is the moral status of any of the others he does? They are simply right to do and not wrong not to do—they are simply supererogatory. To defeat this objection, one would have to maintain—most implausibly—that it is not possible to do any of the extra, unneeded acts. Or one would have to maintain—again, most implausibly—that if it is possible to do some of the extra acts, doing them will not be right.

III. Supererogatory Acts, Not Duties

Even though the assimilation of supererogatory acts to imperfect duties, or imperfect duty fulfilling acts, failed, we have seen that many imperfect duty fulfilling acts are strikingly similar to supererogatory acts. Both sorts of acts are right to do and not wrong not to do. All this is true, of course, of perfect duty fulfilling acts, too. But it is not nearly so plausible to assimilate supererogatory acts to perfect duty fulfilling acts as it is to assimilate them to imperfect duty fulfilling acts.

How are we to account for this? And how are we to distinguish between supererogatory acts and duty fulfilling acts? Can we give a definition of "supererogation" that does not simply, and in an *ad hoc* way, say that no imperfect duty fulfilling act can be supererogatory?

In what follows I shall show that indeed part of the conditions for being a supererogatory act includes (what almost amounts to) an explicit disclaimer to the effect that the act is not a perfect or imperfect duty fulfilling act. In fact, in developing the conditions for being a supererogatory act, we shall develop the conditions (given above) for being a duty fulfilling act. I shall show this using only rightness and wrongness as my moral concepts.

As we have seen we cannot distinguish between a duty fulfilling act and a supererogatory act in terms of the rightness of doing and the wrongness of not doing that act. What condition, then, can be used in the formula

> Act b is supererogatory just in case it is right to and wrong not to do given condition C.

That is, what condition C will distinguish between supererogatory acts and duty fulfilling acts solely in terms of rightness and wrongness?

It might be thought that we could use an insight from the first objection of Sect. II. There the assimilation of supererogatory acts to duty fulfilling acts was argued against on the grounds that any of the supererogatory acts could become a perfect duty. And they could become this simply by being needed to do the requisite number of duty fulfilling acts. Thus we might try

> (1) Act b is supererogatory just in case there is no set of acts such that if none (or all) of the members of that set be done, it would be wrong not to do act b.

This condition has two major interpretations depending on how we take "act." (A) The acts are actual acts—i.e., acts that have been, are being, or will be done; (P) The acts are possible acts—i.e., actual acts and acts that could have been or could be done. I do not think that either (1A) or (1P) will work.

(1A) The problem here is that many if not all duty fulfilling acts would not become wrong not to do simply because some actual acts were or were not done. For even if actual acts were not done, it would be unlikely that any given duty fulfilling act would have to be done to fulfill the duty. Further it is not clear that all supererogatory acts get past (1A). Consider a duty to give a charity ten dollars by the end of the month. Now suppose that one gives the charity ten dollars in the middle of the month and then at the end of the month gives it another ten dollars. Would giving the ten dollars at the end of the month have been supererogatory—or a duty—if one had not previously given ten dollars?

(1P) It should be clear that (1P) will eliminate all duty fulfilling acts. For it surely will be possible to find some set of possible acts such that if none of its members be done the act in question must be done to fulfill the duty. We could simply suppose that that act was the only duty fulfilling act that could be done. However (1P) is too powerful. For it should be clear that supererogatory acts are not necessarily supererogatory; and thus there will be some "moral worlds" defined or constituted by possible acts that must (or must not) obtain for a given supererogatory act to be supererogatory. Consider the supererogatory act of bringing a book to a friend to help him complete his research. Now if one had promised—in the appropriate conditions—to bring him that book, bringing it to him would not have been supererogatory. So much, then, for (1P).

I do not think that there is any need to try to patch up (1), for it can be quickly seen that we cannot divide supererogatory acts and duty fulfilling acts into mutually exclusive sets by considering the following: One and the same act can be supererogatory and fulfill a duty. Consider the duty to give a charity ten dollars. Now suppose one writes it a check for twenty dollars. One has thereby done one act that at once fulfills a duty and is supererogatory.

Given that some acts are at once supererogatory and duty fulfilling, how can we distinguish between such acts at all—let alone in terms of rightness and wrongness? Clearly the answer is that we must not look at the sets the acts form, but rather that we must look at the properties of the acts. And, we must find those properties in virtue of which acts fulfill duties and are supererogatory. Thus we must consider the morally relevant characteristics of the act under scrutiny. We must find out whether it is a token of a duty act type or of a supererogatory act type. Thus we must find out whether it has supererogatory-making characteristics, duty-fulfilling characteristics, or both, to know whether it is supererogatory or duty fulfilling or both. Can we find out all this simply by using rightness and wrongness as our only moral concepts? I think that we can.

There is a problem here: Which properties of the act are morally relevant—which properties do we look for to see if the act is a token of a morally relevant act type? Since most properties could be morally relevant—given the proper circumstances—are we forced to examine all the types of which the act is a token? All that I can say here is that we need consider only those of its characteristics that are, not merely might be, morally relevant. In perhaps a question begging way, I can say that a morally relevant characteristic is one the existence or nonexistence of which entails the existence or nonexistence of a value-making characteristic. Shunting off the original question to one about the nature of value-making characteristics may not be much help. But at least it puts us back on familiar, if not well-understood, ground.

Consider, then, all the morally relevant characteristics of the act in question: $c_1, \ldots, c_n$. Now construct all distinct and nonempty collections of the characteristics: There will be n such collections with exactly one characteristic, $n!/(n-2)!2$ such collections with exactly two characteristics, and . . . , and one such collection with all n characteristics. In all, there will be 2^n-1 collections. Let each of these collections determine—i.e., be the class characteristics of—a set of (possible) acts whose only morally relevant characteristics are those of the class characteristic(s). We can now try

> (2) Act b is supererogatory just in case there is not such a set where it is wrong not to do b if less than some number m of that set be done.

(2) does rule out duty fulfilling acts. But in this it is too strong. As was noted earlier as the second objection in Sect. II, some potentially duty fulfilling acts can be done supererogatorily—after the duty has been fulfilled, of course. To remedy this we can require either that all the acts in that set be dated at a time later than act b, or we can change (2) to read

> (2.1) Act b is supererogatory just in case there is not such a set where it is wrong not to do b if less than some number m of that set be done unless b is at least the $(m+1)$st member of that set to be done.

(2.1) also rules out duty fulfilling acts. Again, however, it rules out some supererogatory acts. Here the problem is that some supererogatory acts also fulfill duties—as noted above. Thus we might try

SUPEREROGATION AND DUTIES 61

(2.2) Act *b* is supererogatory just in case there is at least one such set of acts, where it is not wrong not to do *b* no matter how few members of that set be done.[4]

(2.2) is defective as an explication of, or conditions for, "supererogatory act" since one can satisfy (2.2) by unintentionally instantiating those nonobligatory value-making characteristics in virtue of which an act satisfies it. And while some acts that are right to do and not wrong not to do are adequately characterized by (2.2), supererogatory acts are not. For the nonobligatory value-making characteristics in virtue of which the act is supererogatory must be done intentionally and for their own sake or for the sake of other ends it is right to bring about. That is, not only must the agent be praiseworthy for doing a supererogatory act, he must be praiseworthy for doing what is supererogatory about that act. (I assume here that praiseworthiness can be defined using rightness as the only moral concept.) Thus we should revise (2.2) to

(2.21) Act *b* is supererogatory just in case as in (2.2) and where *b* is done in order to instantiate those class characteristics (at least in part) for their own sake or for other ends right to bring about.

I believe that (2.21) is adequate as an explication of, or conditions for, "supererogatory act." Since we sought (2.21) to find out which characteristics make an act supererogatory or fulfill a duty, we should now give conditions for being such characteristics. Taking our cues from (2.1) and (2.21) this is rather straightforward. Further, giving these characteristics serves another function. As noted earlier, one and the same act can be supererogatory and fulfill a duty. Thus we cannot establish class characteristics for mutually exclusive sets of supererogatory acts and duty fulfilling acts. But in light of these forthcoming characteristics, we can give class characteristics for mutually exclusive sets of acts interestingly similar to supererogatory acts and duty fulfilling acts.

Let us say that a duty fulfilling act is a *pure duty fulfilling act* just in case all of its (positive) value-making characteristics are characteristics in virtue of which that act fulfills a duty. And let us say that a supererogatory act is a *pure supererogatory act* just in case all of its (positive) value-making characteristics are characteristics in virtue

[4] Here I simply ignore the possibility that the characteristic in virtue of which *b* satisfies (2.2) might be overridden. To take care of this, there are well-known and straightforward procedures. I shall not, therefore, do anything to correct this "lack."

of which it is supererogatory. If it is true that every supererogatory act includes a duty—as suggested by "going the second mile"—there will be no pure supererogatory acts. Sets of pure duty fulfilling acts and pure supererogatory acts will be mutually exclusive.

So we can say:

(3) The value-making characteristic v is a duty fulfilling characteristic for act b just in case there is a set of v-instantiating possible acts—as specified for (2)—where it is wrong not to instantiate v by doing b is some number m ($m > 0$) of these acts not be done and where b is at most the mth such act to be done.

Taking our cue from (2.21) we can say

(4) The value-making characteristic v is a supererogatory making characteristic for act b just in case there is no set of acts as specified in (3) and where v is instantiated (at least in part) for its own sake or for other ends right to bring about. Or, it is not wrong not to instantiate v by not doing b no matter how many other v's not be instantiated after b—and it is right and praiseworthy to instantiate v by doing b.

A pure duty fulfilling act, then, is one all of whose positive value-making characteristics satisfy (3). A pure supererogatory act is one all of whose positive value-making characteristics satisfy (4).

IV. Conclusion

I think that it is clear by inspection that (2.1) and (2.21) bear a very close similarity to the early explications of "duty fulfilling act." They clearly bring out the fact that duties are cast or described in terms of act types and are fulfilled by act tokens. This similarity, I believe, serves to confirm the correctness of both the early and subsequent explications.

I think that these explications have borne out my original contentions: (i) There are interesting similarities and dissimilarities between supererogatory acts and duty fulfilling acts; (ii) to bring out these similarities and dissimilarities it is not sufficient to say of the former that they are right to do and *not* wrong not to do while saying of the latter that they are right to do and wrong not to do; (iii) these similarities and dissimilarities are found, or can be couched, in the rather complicated conditions for its not being wrong not to do the former while it is wrong not to do the latter—i.e., roughly, it is not wrong not to exemplify a supererogatory act type, but it is wrong not to exemplify a duty act type; (iv) these similarities and dissimilarities can be explicated using rightness and wrongness as the only moral concepts.

Cornell University

V

Utility and Rights
LAWRENCE HAWORTH

THE question I wish to explore is: What shows that people have rights? Along the way, it will appear that people do indeed have them—not merely legal or customary, but also moral rights (or, to put it another way, a ground for the common and commonly unquestioned conviction that there are such rights will be found); that there are even, in a plausible sense, natural rights; and that among the criteria proposed as grounds for the practice of ascribing rights, three at least—utility, equal freedom, and equal shares—are defensible. The core of the argument, once the spadework has been done, will be that a peculiar significance attaches to the idea of deciding an issue "on its merits": the commitment to proceed in such a way includes a commitment to be disinterested while assessing the alternatives; and, as I shall argue, this latter commitment cannot be met unless one regards the fact that an alternative satisfies the principle of utility, equal freedom, or equal shares as tending to show that it should be adopted.[1]

I. What Is A Right?

When one has a right, what does one have? If we follow the generally accepted analysis of legal rights, we shall say that for every right there is a correlative obligation, borne by another or others, not to interfere with some act one is at liberty to perform. The act which one is at liberty to perform, and with the performance of which another or others are obligated not to interfere, is then said to be one's "right." Being at liberty to perform the act means it is not wrong to perform it, and being obligated not to interfere means one ought not to interfere. As a result, one's right to do something consists in the facts that (1) it is not wrong to do it, and (2) there is someone who ought not to interfere with its being done, in the

---

[1] In developing the argument of the essay I have been helped, in ways that may not be clear to them, by discussions with my colleagues J. S. Minas and Jan Narveson.

sense that by interfering he would wrong the person who has the right.

But when it is asked, "Does anyone really have a right?" ("Are rights anything more than mere conventions?") it is not clear what the question means—even when it is clear what one has when one has a right. It is not at all like asking whether anyone has a pain, and the difference is connected with the fact that, unlike pains, rights are not kinds of things that can be *there*; they aren't events or objects. This leads some to hold that rights are conventions—a view that is generally made to depend on the assumption that unless a belief is descriptive, in the way "my clavicle is painful," is descriptive, or formal, in the way pure mathematics is formal, then it cannot be "true" or "known." If analysis shows that what appeared to be a descriptive statement is really a proposal, then the conclusion will be drawn that no better reason can be given for "asserting" (making) it than for denying it. And the ordinary person's assumption, that it is possible to have as good reason for making a proposal as for believing a descriptive statement to be true, is precluded by the presupposition that in any significant (non-conventional) sense there can be "good reasons" only for descriptive and formal statements.

I think it is true that the "statement" that one has a right is not a statement, but a proposal. When it is said, that a person has a right to do something, this is to be understood as the proposal that he be protected in his efforts to do it, and that others be discouraged in some way from interfering with its being done (or as an endorsement of the fact that people are so protected and discouraged). And the "truth" of the "statement" that he has the right consists in the reasonableness of the proposal. The proposal is reasonable to the extent it can be supported by good reasons. Hence it is important to know what sorts of considerations, if any, could count as good reasons for proposals of this kind.

In their most general form, the required reasons would be criteria of importance for actions, in the sense that they would identify traits of or associated with an act that make it reasonable to regard the act as sufficiently important that one ought to protect the actor in his efforts to carry it out, and to dissuade others who would interfere with its being carried out. In principle, these may be traits of (a) the actors, (b) the world created by the actions, (c) the actions themselves or their maxims, or (d) the world in which the actions arise. The most prominent form of the first is the desert theory of rights, and its most prominent exponent is Aristotle. The second is most obviously (if not exclusively) exemplified by the principle of utility. The third has

E

many forms, but I regard the principle of equal freedom as the most promising one. The fourth could have many forms, but I regard the principle of consent as the most promising one. The desert theory, however, reduces to or is a form of the utilitarian theory (since, with Aristotle at least, the source of merit is contribution to the ends of the city, and to the question, "Why measure merit in this way?" he would seem to have no alternative to answering that it is a practice that contributes to the ends of the city). Consequently, I shall restrict my attention to the other three. Some loss of comprehensiveness results from this decision, since even if the desert theory is a form of utilitarianism it has unique and important characteristics.

II. Principles of Rights: Utility

Consider now the explicit theory that the criterion of importance for actions, which indicates the circumstances in which persons should be supported and protected in their endeavors to act, is utility. We shall say that according to the principle of utility the preferability of a proposed course of action is shown by its promise of having good consequences, where "good consequences" includes at least pleasure (in Bentham's sense of "interesting perception," so that, for example, considered in itself the "pleasure in pain" experienced by a masochist forms a good consequence); satisfaction of actual needs, interests, and wishes: and the fulfillment of goals or purposes. The intent of the classification of kinds of good consequences is that it will permit one to regard as a good consequence any but only those conditions that the individuals on whom they impinge will regard as good consequences. In a secondary sense, of course, one will want to say that conditions productive of good consequences are also good.

Two questions arise in the theory of rights to which one might suppose the principle of utility provides a plausible answer. What kind of reasons, if any, are there for distinguishing among actions and regarding some as matters of right, while withholding even the liberty to perform others? And on what basis, that is in terms of what principle or principles, should the distinction be drawn? The distinction should be drawn, the utilitarian says, because some actions promise to have decidedly good consequences on the whole, while others promise to be extremely harmful in their effects, and it is not unreasonable to expect both that the occurrence of the former sort would be increased if a right to perform them were accorded, and that the occurrence of the latter sort would be diminished if even the liberty to perform them were withheld. And it is obvious that this contains an answer to the second question as well: those actions should become matters of right that promise to have markedly good consequences.

The utilitarian theory of rights (or, what comes to the same thing, of justice) has been objected to in more ways that can be conveniently canvassed here. I shall mention only two such objections. (1) It is said that the principle is arbitrary. Although most people accept some form or other of the principle that the utility of a course of action tends to show that it should be adopted—that utility provides a good reason for adopting it—there is no real basis for this attitude. Thus, Hume: " 'Tis not contrary to reason to prefer the destruction of the whole world to the pricking of my finger." (2) It is also objected that, for example, the enjoyment a rapist experiences tends not at all to minimize the immoral character of what he has done, so that this "good consequence" has no bearing on the answer to the question, "Are there circumstances in which the act would be a matter of right?" In the same way, it is said that utility does not even tend to give one a right to "punish" an innocent person.

One wants to generalize about such cases that the promise of good consequences doesn't count insofar as the act that has them violates the rights of another. But then it does not seem possible to ground the latter rights on consequences, since their distinctive character appears to be that of holding good despite consequences. At least two courses are open. (1) Modify the principle of utility so that it becomes consistent with such rights as that of an innocent person not to be "punished" despite the prospect that good consequences would ensue. This can be done (or attempted) by making the principle apply to rules rather than to individual acts, or by redefining (or more accurately defining) the notion of good consequences, so that, for example, some modes of distribution of goods qualify as good consequences, while others qualify as bad consequences. (2) The second course is that of defining some other (non-utilitarian) principle that is capable of accounting for those rights which we imagine people possess regardless (within limits) of their consequences—one's rights to have debts repaid and promises kept, the right of one who is not interfering with anyone not to be interfered with, the right not to be "punished" for crimes one did not commit. The two principles most often discussed in this connection are the principle of equal freedom and the principle of consent. The first has the effect deriving of rights from characteristics of the act itself, or of the maxim of the act; the second has the effect of deriving rights from characteristics of the world in which the act occurs.

III. Principles of Rights: Equal Freedom

Forms of the principle of equal freedom are found in Hobbes, Rousseau, Kant, Mill, Marx and Engels, Spencer, Popper, and Hart—to mention only those surveyed in Gewirth's useful discussion of the subject.[2] Of these, Hart is most explicit in seeking to derive rights from the principle, and in rejecting a utilitarian derivation.

Hart's avowed purpose is to show that if there are any moral rights, then there must be at least one natural right—the right to equal freedom—where a natural right is defined as a right that (a) all men capable of choice possess, regardless of the character of the society in which they live, and (b) does not arise in consequence of any voluntary transaction into which men enter. This is to argue that one's possessing a natural right to equal freedom is a necessary condition of one's possessing any moral rights, a thesis that will yield the conclusion that there is at least one natural right if it is accepted that people do have moral rights. Hart assumes that this will or should be granted. The significance of the argument in the present context is that it purports to establish a non-utilitarian principle that overcomes widely-felt difficulties in the utilitarian theory of rights.

It appears, however, that Hart makes the rather elementary mistake of establishing, at best, that the right to equal freedom is a sufficient condition (or, in another class of cases, the most prominent in a group of conditions that together are sufficient) of one's having moral rights, but not a necessary one. As will be seen, this is a fatal defect, since one is left with the knowledge that if there are good reasons for ascribing to all men capable of choice a right to equal freedom, then all men have, or are eligible for, moral rights, even rights not derivable from the principle of utility as it is ordinarily understood. But this leads nowhere until, in some other way, the good reasons for ascribing a natural right to equal freedom are produced.

By an equal right to be free, Hart understands that "any adult human being capable of choice (1) has the right to forbearance on the part of all others from the use of coercion of restraint against him save to hinder coercion or restraint, and (2) is at liberty to do (i.e., is under no obligation to abstain from) any action which is not one coercing or restraining or designed to injure other persons."[3]

[2] "Political Justice" in *Social Justice*, ed. by Richard Brandt *et al.* (Englewood Cliffs, 1962).
[3] Hart, *op. cit.*, p. 175.

Hart founds other rights on this right in the following manner. He first distinguishes between special and general rights. A special right is one that individuals have owing to voluntary transactions into which they enter. Thus, promises, contracts, and authorizations create special rights. A general right, by contrast, does not arise out of a voluntary transaction but merely exemplifies in a particular way the right to equal freedom. Examples are the rights to speak and to worship insofar as these acts do not involve coercing, restraining, or injuring other persons, and provided that the person for whom the right is claimed has not entered into a voluntary transaction with another that has the effect of obligating him not to perform the act.

The relation between a general right to do any particular thing that does not involve coercing, etc., others, and the natural right to equal freedom is that of part to whole. It is possible without distortion to define the natural right by saying that adult human beings capable of choice have a right to perform any action that does not coerce, etc., others—from which it follows that each general right is included in the natural right, just as from the fact there is a can containing beans of every color, it follows that the can contains a blue bean. Hart argues that "if there are any moral rights at all, it follows that there is at least one natural right, the right of all men to be free."[4] To establish this, and to show that the natural right is a necessary condition of there being moral rights, he observes that "The assertion of general rights directly invokes the principle that all men equally have the right to be free. . . ."[5] But this is not true. One may base a general right—the general right, say, to worship—on the natural right of all men to be equally free, just as one may defend the view that there is a blue bean in a can by claiming that the can contains beans of every color. But to assert the general right to worship is not to *invoke* the natural right,[6] just as to claim there is a blue bean in the can is not to claim that the can contains beans of every color.

More precisely, Hart bases his contention, that the natural right is a necessary condition of any general right, on the relation that holds between the natural right and general rights. But this relation—that each general right is included in the natural right, or, as he puts it, is a "particular exemplification" of it—implies only that the natural

---
[4] *Ibid.*, p. 175.
[5] *Ibid.*, p. 188.
[6] To claim this is to claim something to which Hart has committed himself—that the natural right is a necessary condition of the general right to worship, so that there is no principle other than the natural right to equal freedom from which the general right to worship may also be derived.

right is a sufficient, but not that it is a necessary condition of there being general rights.

The same case can be made for the relation between the natural right to equal freedom and special rights. Two points must be recalled: first, the transaction that creates a special right is voluntary; second, to have a right is to have authority to limit another's freedom. Hart argues that if we justify limiting the freedom of another on the ground that the other has promised, or consented to, or authorized something, "we are in fact indirectly invoking as our justification the principle that all men have an equal right to be free. For we are in fact saying in the case of promises and consents or authorizations that this claim to interfere with another's freedom is justified because he has, in exercise of his equal right to be free, freely chosen to create this claim. . . ."[7]

But, again, this is not true. One may attempt to justify interference by appealing to the principle of equal freedom, and I shall not dispute that the right that arises out of a promise, say, can be successfully defended in this way, but there is nothing to show that there are not other principles that may be used as well, even in circumstances where the promise is binding despite the fact that the principle of equal freedom is violated. That is, Hart's argument shows that if we assume one has an equal right to be free, then we may infer that when in normal circumstances one makes a promise he creates an obligation for himself and a right in another. For if in normal circumstances (that is, circumstances in which promises are possible) he makes a promise but is not regarded as having created an obligation for himself, and a right in another, then his equal right to be free is denied him. But this is not to show that if one creates an obligation by making a promise he possesses the natural right to equal freedom. For it is open to one to suppose that, say, utility is the ground of the practice of promising, and that each promise is binding (*is* a promise) because it exemplifies sound practice, in which case to claim the right that the promise creates, and the obligation, is to "invoke" the principle of utility, not that of equal freedom.

As a result, the assumption that people possess a natural right to equal freedom makes it possible to argue that they also possess numerous moral rights. But although the principle of equal freedom seems inherently plausible, so that one is strongly inclined to assume it and then, with Hart, deduce moral rights from it, so far no actual account of its plausibility, no explanation of why it is to be assumed, is at hand.

[7] Hart, *op. cit.*, p. 190.

IV. Principles of Rights: Consent (Equal Shares)

The attempt to ground rights to act in characteristics of the world in which the acts occur often finds expression in the endorsement of the principle of consent as embodied in social contract theory. In the recent literature the same approach is exemplified by the theory of justice developed by John Rawls. According to Rawls, the fundamental principles of justice are that ". . . each person participating in a practice, or affected by it, has an equal right to the most extensive liberty compatible with a like liberty for all; and second, inequalities are arbitrary unless it is reasonable to expect that they will work out for everyone's advantage, and provided the positions and offices to which they attach, or from which they may be gained, are open to all."[8]

Rawls associates the ideas of justice and rights in such a way that the foregoing principles are criteria for rights and duties, in the sense that a practice that allocates rights and duties is defensible if, but not unless, it satisfies the principles. The principles diverge from the principle of utility mainly in the requirement that inequalities should work out for everyone's (distributively), rather than a net, advantage. Their similarity with the principle of equal freedom is acknowledged by Rawls, but as will be seen, the real interest lies not in the principles themselves but in one of the attempted lines of derivation of them. In fact, there are at least two such lines of attempted derivation that Rawls interweaves, but one might imagine each of them to be capable of independently establishing the principles. (1) Rawls claims that "These principles [of justice] are those which account for the considered judgments of competent persons concerning the justice of political and social institutions."[9] The reference is to an earlier article,[10] which develops the position that ethical theories and principles are justified insofar as they account for the practical judgments in which a specially constituted panel of "competent judges" concur. (2) Rawls also argues that "the family of principles associated with the concept of justice can be characterized as those principles which rational persons would acknowledge when the constraints of morality are imposed upon them in circumstances which give rise to questions of justice."[11] It is this second line of derivation that gives his theory the appearance

---

[8] "Justice as Fairness," *The Philosophical Review*, vol. 67 (1958), p. 165.
[9] "The Sense of Justice," *The Philosophical Review*, vol. 72 (1963), p. 282.
[10] "Outline of a Decision Procedure for Ethics," *The Philosophical Review*, vol. 6 (1951), pp. 177–197.
[11] "The Sense of Justice," *op. cit.*, p. 282.

of being based on the idea of consent. Development of the theme involves supposing that the members of a society are to attempt to agree on the principles they will use for evaluating and setting up practices, with the understanding that no principles will be adopted that are not unanimously assented to. Then various constraints are imagined to be placed on their deliberations, the principal one being that the participants are self-interested. In the circumstances, this, coupled with the requirement of unanimity, has the effect of assuring that the principles finally agreed upon will endorse a system of practices just in case the system as a whole establishes an equal sharing of risks and of prospects of gain. On one hand, an individual, being self-interested, would not accept a principle that promised to impose on him fewer prospects of gain, or more risks, than the rest. On the other hand, he could not gain acceptance by others of a principle that promised him greater prospects of gain, or fewer risks.

We are confronted then with two ideas, and it is not clear at once which is the more basic. The principles of justice are those principles that could be mutually acknowledged by rational persons subject to the constraints of morality; and the principles of justice are also those principles that promise to establish an equal sharing of risks and of prospects of gain. (1) Rawls regards the first as the more basic, but I would be inclined to say that the second—which I shall refer to as the principle of "equal shares"—is more basic. (2) Moreover, as will be seen, the two principles he calls principles of justice aren't such, by his own criterion—they would not be mutually acknowledged in the circumstances described. (3) Finally, the principle of equal shares is in fact the principle that Rawls is seeking, since this is the principle that would be mutually acknowledged in those circumstances. I shall discuss each of these points in detail.

(1) That the idea of equal shares is more basic than that of mutual acknowledgment or consent may be seen in the following way. The question is raised, "What principles for evaluating practices would be unanimously assented to by individuals who satisfy the conditions of an 'analytical construction' (as Rawls calls it), marked by such stipulations as that the individuals are mutually self-interested, rational, and not envious, and that the principles assented to are to be employed impartially for the settlement of contemporary issues and also for the settlement of future issues the exact nature of which cannot be anticipated?" Then it is intended that one should be able to *deduce* the principles of justice from the analytical construction. But if one asks why each of the stipulations is included in the construction, the answer must be that if it were not included then

principles might be deducible that do not involve an equal sharing of risks and of prospects of gain. The ideas of consent and mutual acknowledgment of principles have no role to play. The issue is not, "What would be consented to?" but "What *could* be assented to, in the specified circumstances?" And what could be assented to is merely what satisfies the conditions implied by those circumstances —the circumstances, that is, delineated by the "analytical construction." But the conditions are such that, taken altogether, no principles could satisfy them except ones that would establish equal shares. Consequently, to say that the two "principles of justice" are those that could be mutually acknowledged is a way of saying that they are the principles that would establish an equal sharing of risks and of prospects of gain.

One might object that this ignores the force of the stipulation that the principles of justice are to be those that could be mutually acknowledged by rational persons "subject to the contraints of morality." That is, the details of the analytical construction result not so much from the consideration, "What set of circumstances will permit the deduction of principles that establish an equal sharing of risks and of prospects of gain?" as they do from the consideration, "What circumstances must be imagined to obtain in order that the persons involved might be made 'subject to the constraints of morality'?" This is true. But then it becomes clear, as the latter question is answered by the description of the analytical construction, that the overriding idea in the conception of accepting the constraints of morality is that of not asking others to take more risks, and not allowing oneself greater prospects of gain; and when it is further assumed that one is rationally self-interested, the additional feature, that one will not willingly accept greater risks and fewer prospects of gain, is introduced. The result is the principle of equal shares.

It might seem, then, that rather than showing the priority of the principle of equal shares to the principle of mutual acknowledgment by rational persons subject to the constraints of morality, this shows instead their identity. I would not object if the following points were granted. First, the idea of actual or even possible consent or acknowledgment has nothing important to do with the latter principle, since when it is said that the two principles are identical what is meant is that the principle of equal shares explicates what a rationally self-interested person submits to when he submits to the constraints of morality. Second, the analytical construction is not to be regarded as a manner of deducing the identity, since the description of the construction itself proceeds with an eye to the fact of the identity, and is regulated by a prior understanding that the constraints of morality involve an equal sharing of risks and of prospects of gain. The analytical construction is then but a way of communicating the fact of the identity.

(2) I wish to argue that Rawls is mistaken in supposing that rational persons subject to the constraints of morality (persons placed in the circumstances described by the analytical construction) must endorse the two principles of justice that he defines. The second of the two principles is the only substantial one, and it has two parts. The major difficulty attaches to the first part of the second principle. It reads: ". . . inequalities are arbitrary unless it is reasonable to expect that they will work out for everyone's advantage . . ." There is a minor problem here that I shall merely mention in passing: The persons concerned would not insist that inequalities work out to their advantage (especially in view of the stipulation that they are not envious), but at most would insist that inequalities do not work out to their disadvantage.

The major difficulty involves the respect in which this part of the second principle is related with the standard interpretation of the principle of utility. The latter principle, it is said, requires only a net advantage, and is objected to on the ground that a net advantage might be attained in a manner that involves an objectionable disadvantage being borne by a minority. Rawls's principle, by contrast, excludes the consideration of a net advantage altogether, in the sense that in terms of his principle a net advantage of any amount would be insufficient to warrant an inequality that does not promise to work out for each and everyone's advantage, or that promises to work out for the disadvantage of at least one. But surely this is too extreme. Although rational persons subject to the constraints of morality would not accept an unqualified principle of utility as the sole rule for evaluating their practices (would not accept net advantage, regardless of its distribution, as the sole criterion), neither would they accept a principle that entirely overrides the consideration of net advantage. In some circumstances the over-all gain promised by an inequality would not seem sufficient to encourage everyone to accept the inequality; on other occasions the over-all gain would seem sufficient. It would depend on the amount of gain or net advantage, on one hand, and on the extent of the disadvantage suffered by the most disadvantaged person (or, in Rawls's analytical construction, the most disadvantaged representative office-holder). If one knew in advance that he would be the one disadvantaged by an inequality, he would not be swayed by the consideration that a net advantage would be gained at his expense. But the second part of the second principle stipulates that "the positions and offices to which [the inequalities] are attached, or from which they may be gained, are open to all." And the result of this is that in advance of the relevant information concerning who will benefit from and who will suffer under any inequality, each must regard a proposed inequality that would result in a net advantage but in disadvantage to a minority (that is, less advantage than is promised by an alternative) as a *gamble*, and must decide whether accepting the inequality would be a good gamble for him by taking into account the chances of his losing (being disadvantaged by the inequality), the extent of his loss if he loses, and his share of the net advantage if he wins (if he is not one of the minority disadvantaged by the inequality). Persons placed in the circumstances of Rawls's analytical construction cannot know in advance what the values for these variables will be in all future issues, and therefore cannot be certain that an option that, while promising to disadvantage some, nevertheless forms a good gamble for everyone, will ever present itself. But neither can they be certain that it will not. And we may add that as a matter of fact good gambles of this sort do frequently present themselves. But then rational persons subject to the constraints of morality would not agree on a principle for evaluating their practices that they knew would forever deny to them the opportunity to accept such gambles.

One example should suffice. Suppose that conscription into the army during a war is entirely by lot, and that being a member of the army involves an inequality *vis-à-vis* civilians. Then I would think that the offices of soldier and civilian satisfy the requirement of openness specified in the second part of the second principle. But some of the soldiers (second lieutenants in the infantry, at least) are ultimately disadvantaged, in the sense that their share of the net gain to their country that is produced by having an army at all is more than offset by the disadvantage they suffer in consequence of their position (they are very likely to be killed), and that this loss is greater than theirs would be under some alternative, for example, the alternative of surrendering without a fight. Thus, all things considered some people are likely to be ultimately disadvantaged by the complex practice of subscription by lot—or by most other ways of forming an army. Consequently, Rawls's second principle condemns the practice. Nevertheless, the persons who become second lieutenants in the infantry, along with everyone else in the society, might reasonably have chosen the practice of subscription by lot—in advance of the actual drawing of the numbers that assigned them their positions of advantage and disadvantage. It is possible to lose a good gamble.

Another way to make the same point is to say that it is possible to have an equal sharing of risks and of prospects of gain in a society that tolerates inequalities that, while producing a net social advantage, work out to the ultimate disadvantage of a minority within the society. This is possible, provided that the positions of advantage and disadvantage are assigned in a fair or reasonable rather than an arbitrary or partial manner, and that the probability of suffering the disadvantage is sufficiently small, or the extent of the possible disadvantage sufficiently restricted, that in view of the share each can expect of the net advantage produced by the inequality—should he be fortunate enough to avoid the disadvantage—he can reasonably assume that choice of the society with the inequality represents a better gamble than does choice of the society without the inequality.

(3) It seems obvious then that the principles of justice defined by Rawls must be revised if they are to be principles to which rational persons subject to the constraints of morality would unanimously consent. The revision should have the effect of making it possible for the principles to endorse practices that promise a net advantage, at the price of disadvantage to some. But the revised principles cannot specify the point at which a promised net advantage would be sufficient to warrant paying the price, since this depends on the values for variables that cannot be known in advance. All that is possible is a principle that delineates the requirement that the system of practices that form a society should represent a good gamble for everyone. But, assuming that two qualifications are introduced, such a principle would be but a form of the principle of equal shares. The qualifications have analogues in Rawls's principles of justice. First, not only is equality desired, but equality at the highest attainable level. This is expressed by stipulating that the risks should be at the lowest point compatible with their being equal, and the prospects of gain at the highest point. Second, a system of practices that embodies an inequality is nonetheless tolerable if (a) it incorporates on balance less risk and greater prospect of gain (for the society at large) than the alternatives, and (b) none who suffers under the inequality (by bearing an unequal share of the risks or of prospects of gain) suffers more than he would under the alternatives. It will be noticed that the effect of these qualifications is to make the principle of equal shares correspond in an important way with Rawls's two principles of justice. It diverges from those principles mainly in that, unlike Rawls's principles, it does not form a criterion for individual prac-

tices, but forms instead a criterion for the system of practices that constitute a society.

Both Rawls and Hart fail, then, in two major respects. Neither succeeds in his project of defending a principle that has, as Rawls puts it, "absolute weight" over the principle of utility. In Hart's case, this results from the fact that, contrary to the requirements of his position, he has managed to establish that the principle of equal freedom is a sufficient, but not that it is a necessary, condition of one's having a moral right. If it were necessary, then no amount of utility would justify one in violating another's right to equal freedom—that right would have "absolute weight." But if it is merely sufficient, then it remains open that one may in the name of utility justify violating another's right to equal freedom; that is, that one may violate that "right" without thereby wronging him, which is another way of saying that in the circumstances it is no right of his, or it is defeated by considerations of utility, or it lacks "absolute weight." In Rawls's case, it is shown by the fact that there may be practices that form a good gamble for everyone, despite their not working out for the advantage of everyone. The second respect in which Rawls and Hart fail is that neither succeeds in accounting for or in grounding the "principle of rights" he proposes.

V. The Ground of the Principles

Nevertheless, the three principles—equal shares, equal freedom, and utility—are all inherently plausible. If in seeking to defend the claim that some action is one's right one were to introduce a consideration the force of which depended on assuming any one of these principles, it seems likely that the consideration would be accepted as relevant to the matter at hand. But how is this plausibility to be accounted for? Two ideas introduced by Rawls are capable of adaptation in a way that is promising in this connection: first, his use of the conception of what follows from one's submitting to the constraints of morality; second, his effort to identify the considered judgments of competent persons as the primitive data of ethics. These two ideas are similar in the respect that in both instances one is encouraged to consider the kind of judgments that would be made by persons placed in a situation that precludes their merely consulting their own interests. But the persons in the first case are nevertheless imagined to have a stake in the eventual decision, so that the requirements of morality have the character of restraints; while in the second case their status is that of disinterested judges whose own futures are not part of the issue. On the other hand, the working out of the first idea —that of submitting to the constraints of morality—involves identifying certain high level judgments or principles as implied by those constraints, so that one who submits to the constraints necessarily accepts the principles; while the working out of the second idea—that of taking the considered judgments of competent persons as the data of ethics—does not involve supposing that the judgments concurred in by the panel are necessitated by the setting in which they operate (in the sense that their not passing just those judgments is proof that they are not operating in the manner contemplated by the definition of the setting; that is, are not functioning as disinterested, competent judges).

Add now, to the conception of such a panel, the idea that in carrying on their deliberations they are submitting to the constraints of morality, in a sense to be explained shortly. Then I think it can be shown, not that any particular judgments concerning particular moral issues are necessitated by that submission, but that certain high level judgments or principles—in particular, at least those of equal shares, equal freedom, and utility—are necessitated, so that unless a person accepts these principles he is not actually submitting to those constraints. Then the actual judgments concerning particular moral issues made by the panel are understandable as results of a conscientious effort on their part to be guided by the principles that their position commits them to accept. It is of course not necessary that they should have a clear notion in the abstract of what those principles are.

In adapting these two ideas of Rawls's it will be useful to drop the stipulation that there be a panel of competent judges, and to replace the conception of submission to the constraints of morality by that of agreeing to discuss an issue "on its merits." The kind of issue that concerns us is that in which someone's rights are called into question; and we are to imagine that a decision-making body (either Rawls's panel or a single individual) commits itself to decide the issue on its merits. For simplicity suppose that a specific proposal is made, and that the problem confronting the decision-making body is that of deciding whether to accept or reject it. In resolving to decide the issue on its merits, the individual members of this body commit themselves (1) to inquire whether there are good reasons for accepting the proposal, and (2) to let the disposition of the proposal be regulated by the outcome of that discussion. Nothing more elaborate than this need be imagined to be involved in the decision to decide the issue on its merits. In particular, no exact notion of what a "good reason" would be like need be assumed, nor need it be assumed that there are good reasons.

In the first instance, the effect of these two very general commitments is wholly negative. Without knowing what one must do, if one is to decide the issue on its merits, one at least knows some of the things one must not do—what not deciding the issue on its merits involves. For there are some rather obvious ways in which one might violate the two commitments. Consequently, one may identify additional commitments of a negative sort that are involved in the initial commitments, and of which it may be said that unless they are kept an issue is not decided on its merits.

I shall mention only two. First, each commits himself not to force a view of his on the others. Thus, there are ruled out physical violence and exceptionally forceful emotional appeals as devices for gaining acceptance of a proposal. Secondly, each commits himself to place his own unique concerns to one side, so that they affect neither the view he evolves during the discussion nor his contribution to it. Each thus commits himself to functioning disinterestedly (that is, he need not be or feel disinterested, but he must act disinterestedly). This is not to say that the distinctive interests of each would not be taken into account, but only that none would allow the fact that certain interests are *his* to bias his contribution and response to the proceedings. Instead, the interests would be regarded as "ones"—to be sure, a "one" who has other characteristics in addition to these interests—so that if they are relevant at all it is for a reason, and the reason would show the relevance of that kind of interests regardless of whose they are, provided only that he possesses the additional characteristics that make the interests relevant.

When individuals discuss a proposal on its merits, so that each contributes disinterestedly, what, in the absence of "subjectivity" and arbitrarily introduced criteria, determines them to reach any conclusion at all? How *can* they be led to some particular view of the merits of a proposal except on the basis of their own interests, needs, drives, etc., or by appealing to criteria that, closely considered, have nothing to recommend them but are arbitrary? When the issue concerns belief of matter of fact, there remain, after personal biases and inclinations are set to one side, sensory experiences that at least *may* permit a settlement of the issue. But it may seem that no analogous material is available when the issue is prescriptive rather than descriptive, so that despite the best of intentions on the part of disinterested decision-makers, their project of deciding an issue on its merits cannot issue in a decision.

Such a position would be fanciful. It is simply a fact that people who discuss proposals do on occasion more or less achieve a stance of disinterestedness and do come to conclusions concerning the merits of the proposals. Observations are passed back and forth, and disinterested people are either swayed or not swayed by them. Nor is there any mystery in this. When a disinterested person is swayed by an observation—finds it to form a good reason in support of some practical conclusion—this can be accounted for by referring to some principle or other that is involved in his stance of disinterestedness, in the sense that his adoption of the stance finds expression in his being swayed by considerations that can be so accounted for. Three such principles are equal freedom, equal shares, and utility. To see that this is so, one need only ask the following question: If a person, purporting to be discussing a proposal on its merits, did not accept as relevant the observations that it would have bad consequences, that it would establish an unequal distribution of freedom (or restrictions), and that it would involve spreading unevenly the risks and prospects of gain, could he be fairly described as functioning in the manner that he purported? Could he be fairly described as functioning disinterestedly? In this connection, the question is not how he feels but how he acts, what the tendency of his actions is. And it is important to notice that one can fail to be disinterested not only by giving undue weight to one's own interests, but also by showing partiality toward others.

I think it is obvious that not to be swayed by observations whose relevance is accounted for by the principle of equal freedom or by the principle of equal shares is to introduce a bias; that is, is effectively to depart from a stance of disinterestedness. For to deny their relevance is to display a readiness to accept a decision that would promote an inequality (either of freedom or of risks and prospects of gain) which one is not prepared to defend by appealing to collateral benefits realized at the cost of the inequality, or to other features of the situation that offset the inequality or minimize its seriousness; and acceptance of the inequality shows partiality for those who are to benefit from it.

The relation of the principle of utility with disinterestedness is rather more complex. A person purporting to be disinterested may effectively violate the principle in three very different ways. One of these is a straightforward example of partiality—he may accept the relevance of some "good consequences," those to himself, say, while denying the relevance of others, those to everyone else. But the other two are, on the surface at least, consistent with the idea of disinterestedness. He may depend on a principle contrary to that of utility, a principle of disutility, or what Bentham called "asceticism," in terms of which one is enjoined to maximize bad consequences; or he may deny that the consequences of a course of action—good, bad, or neutral—are in any way relevant to its preferability.

An elementary consideration indicates, however, that the second of these approaches is a way of showing partiality in just those situations where a utilitarian would find it objectionable. When the consequences of an alternative are good in their bearing on some persons, and bad in their bearing on others, but the good consequences outweigh the bad, so that on the basis of consequences at least the alternative seems reasonable to one who accepts the relevance of utilitarian considerations, then to deny effectively that consequences are relevant at all by not accepting the alternative is to show partiality for those on whom the alternative promises bad consequences. For, not to accept the alternative is, in effect, to assign greater weight to the interests of those on whom the alternative promises bad consequences than to the interests of those on whom it promises good consequences. There are of course circumstances in which, consequences aside, it is reasonable to assign greater weight to the interests of a minority than to those of a majority. But then these are also circumstances in which some principle in addition to the unqualified principle of utility applies, and in which that other principle dominates, so that the situation is not one of denying the relevance of consequences but of acknowledging the force of a more compelling consideration.

But it does not appear that one can condemn the principle of disutility on the same basis. One might hold that to maximize bad consequences is to discriminate against everyone, but it must be admitted that if this is discrimination nevertheless it may be effectively disinterested. However, the relevance of rejecting principles that are incompatible with disinterestedness is that failure to be disinterested implies failure to consider an alternative on its merits. But I think one should say that to choose a course of action because it promises to have bad consequences is to be guided not by its merits but by its demerits. Nor is this merely a bad pun, for although one may *say* whatever one thinks necessary to make a philosophical point, and thus may say that it is a mark of merit in a proposal that it promises bad consequences, if anyone purported really to believe this we would be warranted in concluding that he did not understand the meaning of the term "merit."

The force of this disposition of the principle of disutility will be lost unless it is recalled that nothing is to count as a good consequence that is not regarded as such by the individual on whom it impinges, and that, in the primary sense, everything so regarded because of what it is, rather than what it produces, is a good consequence. As a result, the principle of disutility does not claim that the only consequences that have merit and that show merit in the acts that produce them are those that as a rule people regard as bad. It claims instead that the only consequences that have merit and that show merit in the acts that produce them are those that the people on whom they impinge—including also the person who maintains the principle—regard as bad. The principle, that is, is literally perverse, a circumstance that is also identified by noticing that a sane person who sets about deciding an issue by appealing to the principle and who believes that he is deciding the issue "on its merits" is in fact confusing "merits" with "demerits." It is true, but not relevant, that no one would be so confused.

Even if the foregoing is granted—that the principles of equal freedom, equal shares, and utility are all implicates of disinterestedness—it may still be doubted that there is any significance in the fact. Thus, Alan Gewirth has objected that, "To try to justify an egalitarian, non-discriminatory criterion of justice by an appeal to what would be upheld by an impartial spectator is, obviously, begging the question. For to be impartial is, by definition, to be against discrimination and for equality of treatment."[12] But then if one accepts current views concerning the non-empirical character of philosophy, one could object in the same way to every philosophical conclusion as being question-begging, since whenever the argument is not empirical the conclusion is, or is represented as being, a necessary consequence of some concepts, terms, propositions, etc., in the same way that equality of treatment is a necessary consequence of impartiality.

The important question is whether there is any significance in the fact that commitment to decide an issue on its merits involves commitment to acknowledge the force of the principles of utility, equal freedom, and equal shares. We know that one who does not acknowledge the principles in deciding an issue does not, so far, decide it on its merits. But what of that? What can be said of such a person?

It can be said, subject to one qualification, and in the required sense, that he ought to decide the issue on its merits, and that therefore he ought to acknowledge the principles, since doing so is a neces-

---

[12] Gewirth, *op. cit.*, p. 126.

sary condition of considering the issue in this manner. The qualification is that there are occasions when, owing to lack of information or for other reasons, it seems reasonable to decide by, say, tossing a coin. One may always make a second-level, procedural issue of whether an issue-at-hand is to be decided on its merits, and decide *that* on its merits too. It is with such procedural issues that we are concerned, and with those which when decided on their merits yield the decision to decide the issue-at-hand on *its* merits (rather than by, say, tossing a coin). Whenever this is or would be the outcome of a second-level, procedural issue, the associated issue-at-hand (the settlement of which the procudure contemplates) *ought to be* decided on its merits. It ought to be decided on its merits not because of anything to be accomplished by doing so, but merely because in part the force of saying, in the only sense relevant here, that a course of action ought to be adopted is that it is the course that would be adopted by anyone who decided the issue (of adopting it) on its merits.[13] And since this is so, to say that whenever settlement of a procedural issue on its merits would include the decision to decide the issue-at-hand on *its* merits then one ought to decide the issue-at-hand on its merits, is to say that one ought to do what one ought to do. And one ought.

Part of the force of saying that some course of action ought to be adopted is that it is the course that would be adopted by anyone who decided the issue on its merits. This may be seen in the following way. One who does not decide an issue on its merits acts on the basis of whim or interest. Suppose that such a person tells us we ought to do something, and then supports the directive by saying that he fancies our doing it, or that it would please him or some friend of his, and makes clear that he is unwilling to consider any other "reason." We should conclude that he had misrepresented his position by saying we ought to do that thing. It was not that he really thought we ought to do it, but only that for some reason or other he wanted us to do it. He will not show that he really thinks we ought to do it until, for example, he responds to the question, "Why ought we ?" in a manner that he regards as constituting a consideration of the issue on its merits. In general, to say "you ought to . . . ," as opposed to "I want you to . . . ," or "you'd better . . . ," is to recommend an act as being the one that would be selected following a disinterested investigation of its merits. This point concerning what is involved in recommending an act as the one that ought to be adopted could also be expressed by

---

[13] I say, "part of the force," because "ought to" here is also a directive, while in the case of deciding an issue on its merits the "ought" is replaced by the action that expresses the decision, so that the directive is acted on.

saying that to represent an act as the one that ought to be adopted is to impute to the recommendation that it be adopted a character of objectivity, or that it is to assert that there are good reasons for adopting it that any conscientious person would accept as decisive. When one decides an issue on its merits, one may or may not preface a description of the course decided on with the words, "This is what ought to be done." But given the sense those words have in that context, no other kind of decision procedure produces decisions whose descriptions may properly be prefaced by them. (The procedure of, say, tossing a coin, when this is a reasonable procedure, is an exception—it may be that one ought to do what the result of the toss implies.)

One may object that the argument is purely verbal, that at most it shows that people use "ought to" in the indicated way. The objection seems roughly correct, but does not seem to form an objection. For, it is just this sense of "ought" that one has in mind when he wonders whether he ought to decide issues on their merits, rather than on some other basis. That is, one is not wondering whether he really wants to, or whether it would be better for him to. He can discover, by considering more fully the meaning of "ought," that he ought. There is nothing more to discover. To continue by asking, "But, usage aside, ought one *really* to decide issues on their merits?" deserves the answer: "If by 'ought' is meant what would ordinarily be meant, then one ought—really; while if something else is meant the question can't be answered until it is decided what that something else is."

VI. Natural Rights

To summarize: Acknowledging the force of the principles of utility, equal freedom, and equal shares (at least these) is a necessary condition of considering an issue on its merits. Subject to the mentioned qualifications, issues ought to be decided on their merits, and consequently, the indicated principles ought to be acknowledged. It follows that people do indeed have rights. For, an act is one's right just in case its performance is sufficiently important that others should be restrained from interfering with one's efforts to perform it, and there are acts such that not to regard them as sufficiently important in this sense is to violate and therefore to ignore the force of one or another of the "principles of rights" that have been established. Thus, other things being equal, that one ought to acknowledge the force of the principle of equal freedom involves that one ought to accept the practice of restraining those who interfere with people who are not coercing, restraining, or acting in a way designed to injure others. And this means that the latter ought to be treated in the way people to whom rights are ascribed are to be treated. And so on.

But, also, associated with each of the principles is a right that has most, at least, of the characteristics traditionally associated with natural rights. Thus, associated with the principle of equal shares is a right that everyone enjoys, that does not rest on any political circumstance or voluntary transaction, and that cannot be transferred or abrogated. This is the right to an equal share of risks and of prospects of gain. There is similarly associated with the principle of equal freedom a natural right to equal freedom. And with the principle of utility there is associated a natural right to have one's own interests and concerns assigned the same weight as is assigned to the relevantly similar interests and concerns of others, so that, for example, if some course of action is in one's interest and it is the one that would be selected by the principle, then, other things being equal, that course of action forms one's natural right (there being nothing the individual or anyone else can do to make it not the case that it is his right). The "naturalness" of these rights follows from the fact that the associated principles of rights are absolute, in the sense that not only do they have moral force always and everywhere, but it is not possible for them not to have moral force. This is not to say that each is always applicable, nor that when it is applicable it inevitably dominates other considerations. The terms in which an issue is best put may be such that one or another of the principles has no relevance to its settlement (and so is not applicable). And we have not yet considered the important question of how the principles and others like them are to be adjusted to one another in cases of conflict among them.

University of Waterloo

VI

Let Needs Diminish That Preferences May Prosper

DAVID BRAYBROOKE*

> Things are in the saddle
> And ride mankind.
> *Emerson*

> *Goneril.* Hear me, my lord.
> What need you five-and-twenty, ten, or five,
> To follow in a house where twice so many
> Have a command to tend you?
> *Regan.* What need one?
> *Lear.* O, reason not the need! Our basest beggars
> Are in the poorest thing superfluous.
> Allow not nature more than nature needs,
> Man's life's as cheap as beast's. Thou art a lady;
> If only to go warm were gorgeous,
> Why, nature needs not what thou gorgeous wear'st,
> Which scarcely keeps thee warm. But, for true need—
> You heavens, give me that patience, patience I need!
> *Shakespeare*

Man's own social organization, hitherto confronting him as a necessity imposed by nature and history, now becomes the result of his own free action. The extraneous objective forces that have hitherto governed

---

* This paper was written as a contribution to the values-study project supported at the University of Pittsburgh by the International Business Machines Corporation and by the Carnegie Corporation of New York. It originated as a response to some criticisms by C. E. Lindblom of a related paper on management and the market for public goods, also written for the project. I have profited from discussions with Professors K. Baier, N. Rescher, J. Robison, J. Schneewind, M. Tweedale, and Mrs. Baier, during my tenure of a visiting research appointment at Pittsburgh; I am also indebted to the Departments of Philosophy at the University of Illinois, Chicago Circle, and the University of Illinois, Urbana, at both of which places I read and discussed a preliminary version of the paper; and I wish to thank Walter L. Braybrooke for his comments. I have borrowed from Randall Jarrell, who cites it in the title essay of *A Sad Heart at the Supermarket* (New York, Atheneum, 1962), the quotation from Emerson, though I am told it is so familiar I might have been expected to think of it myself. Even a person with greater powers than mine of recalling poetry, however, could hardly have been expected to think of the quotation from *King Lear* (Act II, Scene 4); I owe it to a splendid feat of *bien trouvé* at Urbana by Professor F. E. Sparshott. The quotation from Engels comes from *Socialism: Utopian and Scientific*.

history, pass under the control of man himself. Only from that time will man himself, more and more consciously, make his own history—only from that time will the social causes set in movement by him have, in the main and in a constantly growing measure, the results intended by him. It is the ascent of man from the kingdom of necessity to the kingdom of freedom.

Engels

CAN men ever escape the dominion of needs, conceiving as they do of new needs perhaps as fast as they invent new means of satisfaction? It is a commonplace of economics that the standard of living is so far conventional that minimum standards of subsistence rise, and thus the scope of ineluctable needs expands, as income rises. But this commonplace calls for investigation. Can we lightly accept changes of convention as enlargements of needs? Matters of need take precedence over matters of preference; if their reach enlarges without limit, little scope will be left for preference. Without imagining what is at issue, men will have foregone a good deal of the new freedom offered them by rising income and technological innovation.

I wish to argue for restraint in enlarging our conception of needs. To do so, I must try to convey what is at issue in this question of philosophical—and social—policy: and to do this, I must venture upon topics so little discussed by philosophers that I shall hardly know what I am talking about. Just what is happening to the concept of needs as technological change rushes over us is something that I can only guess at. The subject of preferences and their evaluation, once considerations of need, consistency and morals have been allowed for, is a philosophical wilderness.

Even the concept of needs itself, in spite of its moral and prudential importance, has attracted few attempts at analysis;[1] the ground has hardly been cleared, let alone rolled smooth enough for dress parades or refined philosophical exercises.

I. Basic Account of Needs, Desires, and Preferences

1. Some of the most important points to be made about needs depend upon a contrast with desires; so I shall begin with desires.

---

[1] F. E. Sparshott's discussion in *An Enquiry into Goodness* (Toronto, University of Toronto Press, 1958), pp. 131 ff., appears to be a pioneer effort. I shall express my unfeigned delight in finding another philosopher in the field with me in the usual philosophical manner, by disagreeing with what he says.

What I shall say about needs and preferences will be founded, as well as I can contrive to found it, on the ordinary language use of "need" and "prefer" and their cognate forms. What I shall say about desire does not have this direct relationship with ordinary language.

"Desire" is a technical term for me, as it has been for other philosophers, whether they have realized it or not; what I say about it is meant to be founded, not on the ordinary use of "desire," but on one branch of the ordinary use of "want." The ordinary use of "desire" falls within this branch, but (especially in the case of the verb "desire") it occupies only a very small and peculiarly distinguished part of that branch.[2]

The things that we literally speak of ourselves as "desiring" tend to be—apart from members of the opposite sex—rather abstract and elevated: happiness—even better, your happiness; variety; solitude; peace; fame; a good name. "I desire to inform you . . ." a general in the field might write, prefacing a communication to his monarch. The monarch in turn might "desire" the general to pursue the enemy. A man may sometimes be said to have "just one desire"—which might be revenge or vindication.

The usage of the verb "want" covers not only these uses of "desire," differing chiefly, I think, in being rather less polite, but much else besides: things not needed, but not spoken of as desired, either; and needs as well. Indeed, the usage of "want" stretches beyond needs, which I think are always in principle capable of being attended to, to ineluctable deficiencies. Thus a woman may want regular features; or a man want agility or imagination or humility.[3]

[2] The tendency of philosophers to extend the use of "desire" as a generalized technical term attains something like maximum visibility in this passage from Hobbes, *The Leviathan*, Book I, ch. 6: "These small beginnings of motion, within the body of man, before they appear in walking, speaking, striking, and other visible actions, are commonly called ENDEAVOUR. This endeavour, when it is toward something which causes it, is called APPETITE, or DESIRE, the latter being the general name." The tendency is further exaggerated (but the upshot not so clear) in Spinoza's definition: "*Desire* is the actual essence of man, in so far as it is conceived, as determined to a particular activity by some given modification of itself," *Ethics*, Part III, Definitions of the Emotions, Def. I. Spinoza also says, "Desire is appetite, with consciousness thereof" (*Ethics*, Part III, note following Prop. IX). In both cases, of course, "desire" is supplied by the English translator; as English translators supply it when rendering Plato and Aristotle. On "desire" being a technical term, cf. Sparshott, *op. cit.*, p. 134. Professor J. B. Schneewind and others brought me to see how limited the ordinary language use is. It is, however, broader than Sparshott allows.

[3] And so may I. So *contra* Sparshott, *op. cit.*, p. 131, footnote 10, "want . . ." does not always mean "I would like . . ." Sparshott himself abandons the doctrine that it does a few pages later, saying, "If . . . I simply say 'I want a new shirt,' the argument (about whether I do or don't) will not get anywhere until I have made it plain whether I really think I need it or have just taken a fancy to it" (p. 135).

Inanimate objects or plants may be found wanting in this way—"You sold me a plant that wants half its roots." Or they may want what they need, as a watch may want winding or a plant want watering. So a child, or a man, may want medical attention; or suitable clothes.

It is another sense of "want" that shares part of its range—but only part—with "desire" as used in ordinary language. In this sense I may want a flashy car; or a country retreat; or a chance to clear my name. N may want turnips with his turkey; a wing-nut to fix the tricycle; the jelly-bean that rolled under the couch. In this sense of "want," only a person or an animal could want something, or want to do something, or want to have something done. A person shows this by making certain efforts, given the opportunity; or by making certain choices; or in ambiguous situations, by announcing what he wants. This is the sense of "want" over which I extend the technical term "desire."

Needs and desires may occur independently of one another. The testimony of the subject less readily establishes the existence or non-existence of a need. Obviously this is so where we speak of watches needing winding, plants needing watering, forests needing rain, lakes needing sources of water. These subjects cannot be said to desire anything, needed or not; and they cannot offer testimony.

But the same points hold for subjects of whom it can be said both that they need and that they desire. The man who needs medical attention may not desire it; or he may desire it and not need it. He can testify that he needs it; moreover, his testimony deserves some weight as evidence. Yet his needs are more objective matters than his desires. They are not more objective because other people can provide for them, and because the fact that other people made the provision would not count against the provision's being relevant and sufficient. Other people may similarly assist in satisfying desires. Nor are needs more objective because other people can establish their existence. Other people can establish the existence of desires, too; they need not, against the weight of other evidence, accept N's contention that he wants to serve his country.

The difference lies in this: in a case where there is evidence that N does desire something, and equally weighty evidence that he doesn't, his testimony will decide the issue, provided at least that we have general grounds for thinking him habitually sincere. But in a case where there is evidence both ways about N needing something, his saying so only begs the question. It carries no more weight than the opinion of anyone else equally observant.

I shall return to the other point, about the mutual independence of needs and desires, later.

2. For subjects of whom it can be said both that they need and that they desire, our language invites distinguishing between two basic categories of needs: *course-of-life needs*, which people have all through their lives or at certain stages of life through which all must pass; and what I shall call "*adventitious needs*," which come and go with particular contingent projects.

Human needs for food, for shelter, for clothing, for exercise, for rest, for companionship, are examples of *course-of-life needs*. So are the need to be suckled, which we all have as babies: and the need, during our prime, for a mate.

Course-of-life needs, though they are connected with possible deficiencies, are not themselves deficiencies; they persist, when the deficiencies connected with them are removed; indeed they exist, even if those deficiencies never occur, being (as may well happen) anticipated.[4] Thus men and beasts need to be fed, short of a certain maximum time during which they can go without food; but if they eat short of that time, which many fortunate beings nowadays normally do, no deficiency appears.

When a course-of-life need fails to be anticipated, a deficiency connected with it will appear, and with the deficiency an occasion for using "need" in a relatively episodic sense. Thus Charlie needs to exercise his neck muscles, having neglected them; thus a man after protracted labor in the hot sun needs a drink of water. When the man has drunk, his need—in this relatively episodic sense—disappears; but as a man he continues to need water and to need an intermittent supply of it, even if he never again experiences a deficiency of it.[5]

I conjecture that agreement about what falls into the category of course-of-life needs will be maximized, as to the number of people agreeing on any given candidate for inclusion, by adopting the following principle of inclusion: course-of-life needs are such that deficiency in respect to them endangers the normal functioning of the subject of need, considered as a member of a natural species. In the case of men, such deficiencies might also be said to endanger health

---

[4] So I disagree with Sparshott's dictum, "Desires and needs are alike deficiencies." See *op. cit.*, p. 133.

[5] In a discussion at Pittsburgh, it was Professor Martin Tweedale who first saw how important it was, in discriminating between senses of "need," to ask whether satisfying the need removed it.

and sanity. By proximately endangering health and sanity, they ultimately endanger survival.

People may differ about what needs health and sanity entail. The scientific discovery that vitamins are essential to nutrition entitles one to say, given that men need food, they need vitamins. People informed of this scientific discovery will subscribe to a longer list of needs than people not so informed. But the accepted list of course-of-life needs may also vary in the direction of becoming shorter. Do men need to mate? Some men seem to be able to get along, sane and healthy, even cheerful, without mates; perhaps all could. The tendency of this objection, even if it is finally rejected, shows that course-of-life needs are not conceptually identical with what psychologists call "drives."[6] People can manage drives so as to escape needing what the drives directly demand.

Course-of-life needs include, besides the familiar examples (or candidates) hitherto given, needs that claim admittance on the same footing, but that are less readily named. Men cannot go on living in health and sanity if they are injured—by accidents, in society or in nature; by deliberate violence. They thus need to be protected against such things; they need at least reasonable precautions against the things that they have reason to fear.[7]

The other basic category of needs contains adventitious needs. Such are the needs of a burglar for a jimmy (so that he can carry through his project of getting the window open); of a householder for a flashlight (so that he can see what he's doing in the attic); of a student for a letter of recommendation (so that he can be considered for graduate school).

Theoretically, these needs admit of a distinction between persistent

[6] Cf. the "hierarchy of basic needs" outlined by A. H. Maslow in ch. 5 of his *Motivation and Personality* (New York, Harper, 1954): physiological needs, safety, belongingness and love, esteem, self-actualization, "the desires to know and understand," aesthetic needs; or see the list of "innate purposive drives" cited from E. C. Tolman in Stephen C. Pepper's *A Digest of Purposive Values* (Berkeley and Los Angeles, University of California Press, 1947), p. 26. I have great respect for Maslow's list of motivating factors; but I note that he does not distinguish between "need" and "desire," as I think he should *at each stage* of his list. I think he should also distinguish between "drive" and "need." Human beings may have an innate purposive drive for sex; but this may be managed (by "sublimation" and other means) so that no need for sex exists. A pitiable solution, no doubt: the point is that one may refuse to accept anything as a need that can be managed and escaped. One would still need the concept of drive or some such concept to explain the effort at management. (Like Sparshott, Maslow confuses "need" with "deficiency": "A basically satisfied person no longer has the needs for esteem, love, safety, etc." *Op. cit.*, p. 105.)

[7] This connection of needs with fears was suggested to me by Pepper's insistence on equal weight for "aversion" and "appetite." *Op. cit., passim.*

needs and relatively episodic ones parallel to the distinction that I drew between course-of-life needs and their episodic counterparts. While he continues in the burglary trade, the burglar goes on needing a jimmy; he needs it even while the deficiency that he might experience without one never occurs, being anticipated by his having a jimmy all along. Similarly, the householder needs a flashlight just in case he may need to go up into the attic, or into some other dark place.

The distinction is thus called for; however, I am inclined to think that the two sides of the distinction are not both so fully realized in the case of adventitious needs as with course-of-life needs. Short-term projects dominate our attention rather than long-term ones, because the short-term projects are readily associated with vividly particularized ends. Getting the window open, or finding the family Bible in the attic, define projects more vividly than being in the burglary trade, or being a householder. Once directed to short-term projects rather than long-term ones, moreover, our attention fastens on episodic needs rather than continuing ones. Short-term projects are liable to end so quickly that one may hardly notice a continuing need for (say) the tool that the given project requires, but that was fortunately on hand all the while. For obvious reasons, we have much more occasion to remark needs that correspond to episodic deficiencies: for tools missing from the toolbox at the time.

There are no counterbalancing reasons, as there are in the case of course-of-life needs, for keeping the corresponding persistent needs in full view. Course-of-life needs, in their persistent guise, constantly demand attention in moral and political discussion; they are staple considerations of precautionary social policy. In their persistent guise, they at least share the spotlight with their relatively episodic counterparts, if they do not steal the scene.

3. Whatever need we consider, in the given categories, its existence is independent of a directly corresponding desire, that is to say, of a desire by the same subject for the same thing. Even if what N needs is something that he needs only adventitiously, because he desires to carry through a particular project, it does not follow that he desires it. He may not know that he needs it, because he does not know that it would be useful; or knowing that it might be useful, he may deny himself the use of it. A man who needs a broom to sweep the verandah may not desire to use it, because he belongs to a caste above that of the sweepers.

If N desires something, he must believe that it is of some possible use to him, however perverse or far-fetched; but believing suffices, knowing is more than the condition requires. Even when the beliefs concern needs, desires do not imply needs; for the beliefs may be mistaken. But the beliefs may not concern needs. N may desire something for his own pleasure, or because of a whim, and freely admit that he doesn't need it.[8]

If N needs something, there is no implication to his beliefs. A man who needs vitamins may not have heard of their existence, much less have come to believe in their usefulness. Hence N does not desire vitamins, though he needs them. But he may also know of a need, even a deep-seated course-of-life need, and not desire to meet it. A man who needs food may refuse to eat. Thus needs do not imply desires, any more than desires imply needs.

Yet all the same it is very often the case that desires engender (adventitious) needs; it is normally the case that (course-of-life) needs give rise to desires, at least when the needs are known. Desires may conflict with needs, as needs sometimes unhappily conflict with one another; but it does not make sense to suggest that they conflict in principle.

Yet it does make sense to say that matters of need take precedence over matters of preference; indeed, I wish to say that this precedence is a fundamental principle of morals and prudence. If N is responsible for M's welfare, then M's needs take precedence for N over N's preferences; and they take precedence for N over M's preferences. Likewise, N's own needs take precedence over his own preferences. The principle supplies a basic standard for assessing people's choices. If people's choices flout the principle, the choices are in error, morally or prudentially.

4. But do not preferences run hand in hand with desires? If it does not make sense to oppose needs and desires in principle, can it make sense to say that needs take precedence over desires? But if it does not make sense to say this, how could it make sense to say that needs take precedence over preferences? Needs and desires so often converge on the same objects—which N wants in both senses of "want"; and to say "I want this" (given a choice of this or that) serves equally well as an expression of desire or of preference.

Yet preferring and desiring can be distinguished. One point of distinction may be found in preferences necessarily being comparative while desires are not. To prefer is to put one thing ahead of another;

---

[8] If N desires something, cannot we always say that he needs this thing to satisfy his desire for it (or he needs it if he is to satisfy his desire)? Perhaps; but it would be very misleading to drop the qualifying expression and say simply, "He needs it." The case may urgently require the comment, "He does not need it."

what one prefers is what one would rather do, or rather have. Neither of the things compared and ranked may be desired, because the choice may be forced. A girl prefers to marry a given man rather than his rival; she may not desire to marry at all.

What N prefers in this instance, all things considered, may not be what N prefers normally, or other things being equal. From the company that she had kept previously, people may have expected that the girl would choose the rival suitor; they did not take into account her family's hopes that they would someday be restored as the royal house of Spain. The rival suitor, though more agreeable, was less royal.

We often say things like "I prefer living downtown to living in the suburbs, but the apartments downtown are too expensive." Even here "prefer" does not mean "desire." I may desire something else entirely—living in a quiet village by the sea, but the conditions of my employment prevent me from considering this alternative.

N's saying that he *would* prefer x to y may be intended to contrast the tastes that he might have if he were an Arab rather than a middle-class, suburban American; or to contrast what he normally prefers to what he prefers, given the special circumstances of the present instance; or to indicate politely his inclination in the present instance, simultaneously undertaking to hear any comments that might forestall following his inclination.

But saying simply, "I prefer x to y," already leaves this polite opening for comments—though not quite so wide open. Thus it is not always determinate beforehand whether "prefer" means "prefer in this instance, that is all things considered" or "prefer, other things being equal" (or both). Only after the agent has actually chosen can we surely infer what he prefers, all things considered; up to that point, what he prefers may always be something put aside in deference to stronger considerations.

The principle of precedence for needs over preferences implies that if there is a choice between x and y, and x is the object of a need, while y is not, then the choice is not to be determined merely by comparing x and y *ad hoc*, which might suffice for arriving at a preference between them. The fact that x is needed upsets (for a prudent or a morally conscientious person) any previous inclination to prefer y, and forestalls further consideration.

However, may it not be the case that x and y both are needed? Needs sometimes conflict, and one must choose between them. But forced choices of this kind would not be described in ordinary language as "matters of preference." One would not say, "I chose x

rather than *y* because I preferred *x*"; to speak this way would treat the case too lightly. One would say, "I had to give up *y*, though I needed it (or, though *M*, my ward, needed it)"; one might explain, "I had no choice but to give up one or the other, *x* or *y*." One's preferring *x* would then be irrelevant; the moral or prudential question would be, which of the conflicting needs was then most urgent.⁹

Needs often admit of a variety of means of satisfaction. Which means to choose may then be a matter of preference; if preference in this matter should conflict with need in another, the principle of precedence requires that the preference give way. Schematically, assume that *x* or *y* or *z* are equally means of meeting one need, while *t* or *u* or *v* are means of meeting another. *N* prefers *x* to *y* to *z*; but taking *x* entails foregoing *t* and *u* and *v*, while neither taking *y* nor taking *z* entails this. The needs, again, may be *N*'s own, or his ward's, or some combination of the two. The principle of precedence requires that *N*'s preference for *x* give way to the second need. I need food; but my preferences for eating *pâté de foie gras* to the sound of trumpets gives way to my needs and my family's for food and clothing and a lot of other things, none of which can be obtained if I indulge my tastes for heavenly dining; I reconcile myself to minced collops and canned spaghetti.

The difficulty about needs taking precedence over desires can now be disposed of. Needs and desires are not opposed in principle; yet if having *x* is a matter of desire without being a matter of need, and it is incompatible with having *y*, which whether desired or not is needed, then having *x* gives way to having *y*. Needs thus take precedence over desires in much the same way that they take precedence over preferences. It is equally a moral or prudential error to flout the principle of precedence in either connection.

⁹ One's preferring would be irrelevant or empty. I do not wish to deny that "prefer" can be generalized, as the economists generalize it, so that every choice implies a preference, at least a preference all things considered. I have thought in the past that this generalization was supported by ordinary language; but choice-situations like those just described, in which needs conflict, make me think again. Here preferring *x* seems not just empty, an inference from a choice motivated not as a matter of preference, but otherwise; preferring *x* does not seem to enter the picture naturally at all. It would at best have to be extracted by dialectic. Whether one generalizes "prefer" or not, as the economists do, one must keep in mind the principle subordinating matters of preference to matters of need. The economists do not, which is one thing that inclines some of them to think that there are no intersubjective grounds besides consistency for criticizing preferences, and others of them to think there are no grounds besides consistency and a principle of not harming others. (Such a principle might concede part of what the principle of precedence for needs demands, but not by any means all of it.)

Are the needs to which precedence is to be given necessarily course-of-life needs? The principle has most emphatic effect, morally or prudentially, when it is applied to course-of-life needs. These are preeminently the needs which a guardian, for example, must provide for in providing for the welfare of a person under his protection. But I believe that the principle reaches further, extending from judgments of imprudence to judgments of irrationality. If N has adopted a certain project, he has committed himself to meeting certain needs; adventitious though these needs may be, it is irrational to jeopardize meeting them by treating the associated choices as mere matters of preference.

5. It must not be thought that because what we prefer may be something in itself unimportant, or because our preferences may be set aside by stronger considerations, that preferences do not command respect. In the first place, the fact that the alternatives open within a particular sphere of discretion are unimportant is no excuse for taking away the discretion. If the alternatives are trivial, what matters but having the discretion? If they are not entirely trivial, then how could having discretion escape mattering a good deal?

In the second place, respect for preferences may be admired as displaying a delicate feeling for liberty. Just as to say, "Your wish is my command," is to undertake, in delicate supererogation, to do much more than heed your commands (whatever commands you are entitled to make)—to anticipate what you cannot command or might not command were you entitled to, so respecting preferences implies renouncing on our part any final obstructions to your exercise of liberty. No doubt we may try to dissuade you; we may recount drawbacks and offer alternative attractions; but finally, if we are to be consistent with our undertaking, we must withdraw. Trivial or not, in our eyes, in our eyes sensible or whimsical, misdirected, and perverse, your preferences—not ours, or our wants or desires—are to be decisive.

II. Three Problematic Aspects of Enlargement in Needs

1. The basic account that I have given of the concept of needs already allows for two sorts of novel application, neither of which seems objectionable, and neither of which seems to modify the concept itself.

There are, in the first place, discoveries to make about the causal requirements of course-of-life needs. Men need food; but this need leaves much to discover, as the past couple of centuries have shown, about specific needs for varieties of food, as for food rich in vitamins. The novelty of saying that men need vitamins does not consist, however, in introducing a new heading (parallel to "food") under course-of-life needs. Without shifting or stretching the concept of needs, the discovery about vitamins leads simply to filling in a detail under an existing heading.

In the second place, men are continually embarking on new projects of various kinds, and thus bringing new adventitious needs forward for recognition. If one is going to play ping-pong, one needs a ping-pong table, and a number of other things, which perhaps one never spoke of needing before. Here, headings multiply as fast as the new applications of the concept; but the concept does not change. So long as the new applications are firmly associated with particular contingent projects, the concept already has laid out room for them as adventitious needs.

Objections easily produced keep the first sort of englargement in needs within control by demanding warrants drawn from accepted course-of-life needs. Objections sufficient to exercise reasonable control over the second sort of enlargement, one might think, would be readily forthcoming in criticisms of the projects that the needs in question are associated with.

2. How, then, does it happen that there is any trouble about enlargement? The trouble is conceptual, arising not from applying an unchanged concept to new cases, but rather from distorting the concept to embrace dubious applications. These applications take place in an indistinct logical space lying between the categories of course-of-life needs and adventitious needs. Assigned firmly to neither of the basic categories, the needs or supposed needs falling in this region often acquire without due critical resistance more of the force of course-of-life needs than they deserve.

The trouble is complicated in origin. To represent it in detail, I shall first distinguish three problematic aspects of the application of the concept of needs; then I shall call upon this three-part distinction in expounding a hypothesis about enlargements of application. It is primarily the enlargements that are problematic; the aspects are problematic because of the enlargements that occur under them.

The first aspect of application to notice has to do with the variation at any given moment as to the needs ascribed to different persons. The paradigms of course-of-life needs are needs that men have universally. But I think we are prepared to admit that some people may need peace and quiet and opportunities for solitude, while others do not; that if some people can make do with celibacy, other people need sexual outlets; that some people, notoriously, need drugs, while most people fortunately do not. These variations in needs correspond in part to innate differences in physical and mental constitution,[10] just as course-of-life needs proper correspond to innate similarities. In part the variation depends on socially induced differences, as a need for drugs, though it may now correspond to a difference in physical and mental constitution, originates in the temptations of a milieu and the persuasion of others.

The link with physical and mental constitution gives these variations in needs a foothold on the threshold of course-of-life needs; perhaps a foothold inside, if not a place at the paradigmatic center. So far as a need by variation affects health and sanity it has the same footing as a course-of-life need. Course-of-life needs themselves do not all require (as we now understand them) a physical basis; it suffices, for example, that by mental constitution men need companionship for us to count this as a course-of-life need. Turning to variations of need, we might accept from the psychoanalysts the suggestion that some people have a need for self abasement, without by any means prejudging the question whether the implied difference in mental constitution has a physical basis.

A second aspect of application in which the concept of needs becomes problematic reveals itself in connection with the subject of social status. The struggle to keep one's place in society (and for some people to maintain normal progress upwards) seems to entail various needs or supposed needs. In the United States, in the urban and suburban middle-class, it is obvious very nearly beyond question that N must have certain skills, acquired through education; that he must belong to certain organizations, or at least be eligible for membership, that he needs certain material possessions—a telephone; a house with an indoor toilet; clothing of narrowly limited sorts; a car; a refrigerator.

Are these—and the variations in them—course-of-life needs, or on the threshold of being such needs? They are not so closely connected with health and sanity. Failing to meet them would mean discomfort; but lots of people, even in the United States, bear such discomfort. Failing to meet them would mean embarrassment; but people normally retain health and sanity even in the face of embar-

---

[10] Like the differences of body-types that W. H. Sheldon treats in *The Varieties of Temperament* (New York, Harper, 1942) and other works.

rassment. Moreover, people vary a great deal in what they subjectively regard as essential to preserving their status; but no needs are merely matters of subjective reckoning, and course-of-life needs do not depend on personal projects.

Yet there is an analogy between keeping one's place in society and surviving physically. People may fear loss of status, or what they deem loss of status, as much as they fear physical extinction (or more). Loss of status may make life "not worth living" in their eyes; the end of one's career, disappearance from one's accustomed place, "dropping out of sight," may seem so many approximations of mortality.

Furthermore, the two modes of survival are connected not merely by physical survival being a necessary condition of the other, but also by social survival being an object of pursuit to which physical survival attaches. Most people, in a society where the division of labor is as complex as it is in ours, do not pursue physical survival directly, or often even think of it as something to work for. They strive instead to keep their jobs—their places in the social network of roles that furnishes an overall provision for physical survival. Physical survival is an incident of social survival, and hence not neatly separable.

The third problematic aspect of the application of "needs" that I wish to mention is manifested in the course of social change. The needs or supposed needs entailed by social survival differ from role to role and class to class at any given time; but they also vary over time as society undergoes conquest and diffusion, or undertakes technological innovation, the chief cause of rising social income. Of these varieties of social change, technological innovation and its consequence, rising social income, currently offer the most familiar invitations for new applications of the concept of needs.

People whose fathers walked to work, or commuted by train, now (so they say) need cars to get there, because they live so far away, and outside the reach of public transportation; maybe (so they say) they need second cars, because otherwise their wives cannot do the shopping, or visit friends. People who once got along with iceboxes now—without extravagance—say they need refrigerators, and not merely refrigerators, refrigerators that are half freezers.

Besides envisaging needs for the specific new products of technology, people expect, with the rise in income caused by technological change, to have larger quantities of various products new and old. Their notions of the quantity of hot water to be on tap at home, for instance, or of the amount of medical attention to be available, enlarge, and in enlarging, tend to extend the application of the concept of needs.

3. The basic two-category account of the concept of needs, taken together with the account just given of three aspects of extended application, gives an approximate picture of what may be called the structure of the concept of needs in ordinary language. Concerning this structure, I wish to put forward a three-part hypothesis: (1) that the structure is such as to invite not only overextension of the concept of need, to matters that could well be regarded otherwise, but also the assimilation of newly conceived needs to course-of-life needs rather than to adventitious ones; (2) that not only does the structure invite overextension and assimilation of this sort—both actually occur; (3) that by occurring, overextension and assimilation inhibit the exercise of freedom in the development of preferences.[11]

I have no good way of estimating how important this process is, by comparison with other possible processes leading to similar inhibitions. Very likely social pressures lead people to treat some wants with the same priority, care, and sense of compulsion that they treat needs, without leading them to conceive of these wants as needs. All I contend is that if (as I suppose) the process of overextension and assimilation does occur, then it contributes something to inhibiting the free exercise of choices and hence the free development of preferences.

There would be little or no trouble about inhibition if incoming suggestions about needs newly to be recognized were firmly sorted out between the two categories of the basic account; and if new assignments to the course-of-life category were continually minimized relatively to new assignments to the adventitious category. Needs in the adventitious category obtain precedence only when the projects that they are associated with are accepted; and the projects clearly are contingent ventures, which are open to straight forward criticism.

---

[11] If (1) is true, then the clarifications attempted in this paper may be held to be an instance at least of prophylactic positivism; if (3) is true, it can be considered a contribution to therapeutic positivism as well. (2) may be regarded as implying an instance of either, or of both.

(1) is the only part of the hypothesis that lies substantially within my province as a philosopher; it requires empirical evidence, but the evidence may best be gathered, one might contend, by essentially philosophical methods, i.e., by dialectic with other speakers of the language, rather than by a take-it-or-leave-it questionnaire of public opinion. Parts (2) and (3) require further sorts of evidence that a philosopher is not in a position to gather systematically. I put them forward to show the significance and motivation of my discussion, and to sharpen its edge.

According to the hypothesis, however, this firm sorting does not occur. People are not mindful of the structure of the concept of needs and do not observe the division between the basic categories. New applications of the concept are undertaken and accepted without being assigned to either of the basic categories, or even accounted as forming new distinct categories of their own.

Furthermore, new applications, which firm sorting would have assigned to adventitious needs (given only the two basic categories to choose between), gravitate to the threshold of course-of-life needs. Here the hypothesis covers (I think) a very complicated process, which may be outlined as follows:

Anything spoken of as a need, without explicit qualifications attached, tends to obtain something of the force of course-of-life needs, which do not demand qualifications. But a gravitational process also operates. Incoming suggestions, brought in say by technological change and rising income, and thus figuring in the third aspect of extended application, are offered without qualifications. People say simply that they need a car, or need a refrigerator. The suggestions are accepted, more and more widely; quite quickly during a period of rapid technological change, they shift to the second aspect of application, and become assimilated to needs entailed by social survival. Because social survival and physical survival cannot readily be separated as objects of pursuit, there is a direct route for the newly accepted—perhaps too easily accepted—needs to gravitate toward being assimilated to course-of-life needs. There is also an indirect route toward the course-of-life category by way of the first aspect of application—the variation of needs between people of different physical and mental constitution. This variation and the variation of needs between people of different social position tend to run hand in hand and merge in casual thinking; and the variation associated with differences of physical and mental constitution has, as we saw earlier, much the same footing as course-of-life needs, likewise connected with physical and mental constitution, and likewise (in some cases) not demanding a strictly physical basis.

A complex pattern of attractions operates, therefore, on the course-of-life side of the indistinct region within which problematic new applications of the concept of needs are introduced. There are no equivalent attractions on the other side, the side of adventitious needs. On the contrary; the most visible examples of adventitious needs are the relatively episodic ones, attaching to vividly defined short-term projects. These resist attempts to assimilate to them needs attaching not to projects, but to ways of life—needs that may perhaps be replaced by others, but that are logically persistent with a way of life so long as this continues. But the persistent department of adventitious needs is dimly lit, and easily overlooked. So incoming suggestions, in more than reasonable numbers, are attracted into the pattern surrounding course-of-life needs.

III. Liberation and Assessment of Preferences

1. The beginnings of practical resistance to the overextension of needs may lie in person by person application of the obvious lessons of the preceding account of the concept. If a person bears in mind the structure of the concept of needs, with its liability to overextension and to distorted assimilation, then he will confront incoming suggestions about needs more skeptically. He will also be in a position to sort accepted suggestions more firmly. Applying his knowledge of the structure of the concept, he can assign the suggested extensions to one of the basic categories of need or to a distinct new one. Thus he can go beyond merely defensive skepticism; he can fulfill the conceptual demands of new contingencies and new challenges to adaptation.

Person by person resistance, it is important to see, can be efficacious. Everyone has some scope for revising easy suggestions—other people's or his own—about needs; and changing his budget of time, effort, or money accordingly. With the change, so much in the way of resources will have been saved from the clutch of needs and put at the disposal of preferences. Some of the changes may be large, compared with a person's whole budget; an accumulation of small changes might transform the budget and revolutionize his way of life. If many single budgets changed in either way, the effects on the composition (and perhaps the size) of social output might be considerable.

Nevertheless, the efficacy of person by person resistance is limited, and the costs of engaging in it are sometimes so formidable as to deter the substantial numbers of people whose resistance must occur if the system of supposed needs is to be changed. People cannot, acting singly, person by person, hope to do much about the automobile and the far-reaching social arrangements—for living; commuting; shopping—that presuppose every family (or nearly every family) having a car. To make an important difference to the car and suburb and supermarket system people would have to take concerted action—for example, through existing organs of government, or perhaps through new agencies for social planning.[12]

2. The remedy for overextending the concept of need and lending doubtful new applications of it undue force cannot then be left entirely to single persons, acting as individual consumers. But neither can the general purpose that remedy is to serve be entirely confined to making more room for private consumption, sometimes by relying on personal resistance, sometimes by arranging for concerted action. At any rate, an inadequate picture of what is at issue in the overextension of the concept of needs results from assuming that even concerted actions would only be designed to promote private consumption.

Approaching preferences through an account of needs, one naturally sees preferences in the perspective of the individual consumer. But then, once the principle of precedence has been allowed for and needs duly taken care of, it appears—in that perspective—that nothing but consistency and avoiding harm to others remain as principles for assessing preferences. The economists' theory of consumer behavior assumes, in fact, only the principle of consistency; the other principles may however be superimposed. When the other principles have been satisfied, the economists' theory would appear to apply without possible objection. It appears that everything that remains to be budgeted for will be a matter of personal preference, to be determined by comparing the relative marginal intensities of different preferences under the caution that the results should be consistent. Thus the alternatives of more expenditure in the public sector—on education, rehabilitation, parks, conservation—or more in the private sector[13] will figure as items in personal budgets, some consumers preferring to consume relatively more in the public sector, some consumers preferring to consume relatively less, both sets voting accordingly (when they have a chance).

More hangs on these alternatives, however, than the economists' representation of the perspective of individual consumption takes notice of. The choice between supporting activity in the public sector and refusing to support it may involve a choice between ways of life:

---

[12] Government may not—at any level—be the most suitable vehicle for concerted action in all cases. I do not wish to deny, furthermore, that grave problems arise about which organ or level shall be selected, when it does seem best to work through government rather than outside. (An example of working outside may be found in the method suggested in Skinner's *Walden Two*, of groups of convinced people retiring from the society around them into their own specially designed communities. It is an extreme method, but a time-honored one.)

[13] Galbraith's alternatives in *The Affluent Society* (Boston, Houghton Mifflin, 1958).

between, for example, a life like the life of Athens in Pericles' vision, where memorable efforts in civic aesthetics compensated for frugal private lives; and, on the other hand, the way of life exhibited in many prosperous conurbations in the United States, where gadgets accumulate inside the picture windows, and waste and litter outside —in Galbraith's phrase, "private affluence, public squalor."

Perhaps one may speak of preferences between ways of life, and represent them in individual consumers' budgets; but preferences of this kind demand special attention of a sort that they do not usually get from economists. They are, one might say, second-order preferences, which do not have the same footing as preferences for tea over coffee, for tape-recorders over player-pianos, or even for more gadgets over more taxes for education. Particular preferences like these manifest preferences for ways of life; and at least when the latter are established and conscious, they will determine particular preferences.

They will also operate as reasons or principles for judging particular preferences as worthy or unworthy. One possible objection to the preferences that a given person expresses lies in their not manifesting a second-order preference for a noble and attractive way of life. Naturally, people who do not share this second-order preference, conceiving a noble and attractive life in different terms or waiving the consideration entirely, may not find the objection arresting; but perhaps they would respond to an objection (or vindication) resting on some other second-order preference. The important thing to see is that there are ideas at this level that can be drawn upon to criticize preferences.

The notion of second-order preferences is not entirely adequate for representing such ideas, however. We may think of controlling the extension of the concept of needs so as to gain some freedom for developing second-order preferences simultaneously with expressing particular preferences that would otherwise be displaced by needs. Before the second-order preferences are fully developed, however, general schemes of orientation operate over particular preferences and direct them more or less definitely. These schemes may in time issue in second-order preferences; meanwhile, they operate without being preferred or chosen themselves and without being represented by any explicit second-order preferences or deliberate overall choices. They are rather fallen into, during a process of social persuasion and personal experimentation. A second-order preference, if it ever comes to expression explicitly, will be something long foreshadowed by an operating scheme of orientation, which has inspired a series of experimental preferences and been strengthened by a series of experimental successes. Besides ideal ways of life, such schemes include ideals respecting activity within specific vocations; and also ideals having to do with the dramatic pattern of cumulative activity exhibited in lifetime careers.

When a person adopts a vocation, conscious of the accomplishments possible in it, ambitious to excel in those accomplishments, he adopts an ideal of activity. A physician, to fulfill this ideal, must be alert, prompt, imaginative in dealing with patients; scrupulous about medical ethics; constantly improving his skills. The would-be physician, accepting this ideal, will not expect to have much leisure; nor to be free to indulge himself in food, drink, or the pursuit of his female patients. Hence the ideal drastically circumscribes the kinds of consumption that he might otherwise engage in, given the generous income that medical success attracts. The ideal also guides particular —first-order—preferences on matters inside and outside the sphere of private consumption that are less critical to the physician's vocational performance: for example, votes on questions of hospital financing or international scientific cooperation. Other vocations will guide and circumscribe preferences differently. A politician may well have different preferences regarding hospital financing, or about hospital organization, as it affects service to the public. Conformably to his vocation, a politician will spend a lot of time, which a surgeon would not spare, patiently listening to miscellaneous other people.

Associated with the choice of vocation one often finds the choice of a career, that is to say, of a pattern of development in a vocation. Thus an aspiring businessman expects to begin—say, during summer vacations from college—as an apprentice on the factory floor; then, shifting about from one operation to another, to learn the ropes as a junior executive (or to begin making the first ventures into business on his own account); next, to prove himself in a first major responsibility or undertaking; then to double and triple the scope of his power until he becomes a captain of industry; finally to engage in active philanthropy and civic leadership.

Ideals regarding specific vocations and careers reveal, furthermore, the operation of general ideals of character and general life-history-ideals. To some vocations, the character of "le chevalier sans peur et sans reproche" is appropriate; to others, the character of (say) the Quaker townsman, the man of peace and probity. Life-history-ideals appear at their simplest (but most widely and deeply cherished) in the desire to pass adequately through all the stages of a normal life: infancy, youth and freedom; romance; marriage; child-rearing; free middle age; retirement; grandparenthood. They figure more ambitiously in grand designs for spectacular accomplishments meeting dramatic challenges, as in careers climaxing as a virtuoso, a big-leaguer, a captain of industry, a Nobel prize-winner.

Use of these ideals to assess the choices in which preferences are expressed—and also to assess the desires in which the choices originate—raises questions of ultimate importance about the meaning of life—about what life amounts to—about making something out of life. People whose preferences are not governed by any character-ideal or life-history-ideal at all will be thought to be wasting their opportunities for making something of their lives. People who pursue character-ideals or life-history-ideals inapposite to given circumstances will be thought irrational. People whose character-ideals or life-history-ideals do not consort with the interests—or the convictions—of others will be called on to change to more suitable ones. Different societies may be more or less liberal in this connection; but every society has some such ideals, offered in principles for the art of living.

3. What is at issue in the overextension of the concept of needs and the undue force ascribed to doubtful new needs can now be more fully stated. Overextension and misassimilation frustrate the use and development of general schemes of orientation for preferences—among them ideals of vocation and character; and ideals respecting careers and life-histories. To develop fruitfully, these schemes require freedom for experiments with preferences, for they flourish only by demonstrating, in sequences of experience and discussion, the attractions of the combinations of preferences that they inspire.

People may think of themselves, in the long-term perspective of their lives and activities, as pursuing ideals of the kinds mentioned; but if they are preoccupied with needs or supposed needs in the ways described, the perspective of consumption will dominate them. They will miss opportunities to carry out projects inspired by the schemes of orientation that they possess, so far as they possess them. They will also miss opportunities to modify, elaborate, and enrich their ideals by personal invention.

As received, the ideals are sketches only—sketches, as it happens, continually threatened with obsolescence by technological change. Mechanical or computerized methods displacing traditional human skills have widely undermined the ideals of vocation and career inherited from the past. The undermining will go further. New ideals

—new schemes of orientation—are urgently needed. They will not be discovered, or become effective, if preferences do not gain more freedom than the uncontrolled extension of needs will allow.

Dalhousie University

VII

Whewell's Ethics

J. B. SCHNEEWIND

WHEWELL's ethical theories[1] have suffered much more from neglect, impatience, and misinterpretation than his theories concerning science. The latter at least were taken seriously and widely discussed during his life-time, but even his close friends did not like his ethical writings. "For my own part," Todhunter says, "I think his writing is very good, vigorous enough to interest and so clear as to prevent any misunderstanding. I except, however, the *Elements of Morality* in which the author's power seems for a season to have deserted him."[2] John Stuart Mill used and admired Whewell's work on the history and philosophy of science, although he disagreed very heartily with much of it. But he could find nothing better to say of Whewell's major work on ethics than that it was a mere "catalogue of received opinions . . . one of the thousand waves

---

[1] Whewell's main writings on ethics are as follows. I give in parentheses the abbreviations to be used in future references:
a. *On the Foundations of Morals. Four Sermons* (Cambridge and London, 1837). (*FM*)
b. *Elements of Morality, including Polity* (Cambridge, 1st ed., 1845; 2nd ed., 1848; 3rd ed., with an important supplement containing a chapter of replies to criticisms, 1854; 4th ed., 1864). (Todhunter says that "the work assumed in the second edition the form which it permanently retained." I. Todhunter, *William Whewell, D.D., An Account of his Writings*, 2 vols. [London, 1876], I, p. 249.) All references in the present essay are to the fourth edition, and are by *paragraph*, not by page number, to facilitate the use of other selections. (*EMP*)
c. *Lectures on Systematic Morality* (London, 1846). (*LSM*)
d. *Lectures on the History of Moral Philosophy in England* (Cambridge, 1852; 2nd ed., 1862). The second edition, which is used here, contains supplementary lectures not printed in the first edition, and paginated separately. The first twelve lectures were delivered in 1838, the next six, all on Bentham, were added when the first twelve were published. Thus the original lectures antedate the publication of *EMP* by seven years, which may account for the vagueness of the theoretical introduction to ethics given in the first of them. (*Hist.*) (Where reference is made to the separately paged additional lectures, the references will be: *Hist. Add.*) Todhunter lists *Two Introductory Lectures to Two Courses of Lectures*, 1841, among Whewell's moral writings, but I have not been able to examine a copy of this work.

[2] Todhunter, *op. cit.*, I, 412. And see the very critical letter from the Rev. F. Myers, dated July 31, 1845, in Mrs. Stair Douglas, *The Life of William Whewell, D.D.* (London, 2nd ed., 1882), pp. 322 ff. Whewell's reply (pp. 325–330) is useful.

on the dead sea of commonplace."[3] James Martineau, himself, like Whewell, an intuitionist and defender of religion, found it necessary to condemn Whewell's ethical writings in unusually harsh language, calling them "preposterous," "absurd," "superstitious," the results of "moral affectation" and "verbal legerdemain": the *Elements of Morality* he described as not so much philosophy as a "premature result of an aversion to the conclusions of Locke and Paley."[4] It is perhaps not surprising that there have been no serious studies of Whewell's ethics since the discussions by Martineau and Mill. But the neglect, though understandable, is unfortunate. Whewell was responsible for the revival of the study of moral philosophy at Cambridge, and he was the first of a line of Cambridge moralists—John Grote, Henry Sidgwick, G. E. Moore, C. D. Broad—whose outlook, despite important differences, is strikingly similar on certain central issues. A knowledge of his work is therefore important for an understanding of the history of English moral philosophy. It must be granted that the style of Whewell's ethical writings is poor, the arguments often incompletely stated, the premisses sometimes lacking, and the connections between propositions too frequently obscure. Still, a sympathetic reading of his work in the light of his general theory of the nature and progress of knowledge[5] reveals the outlines of an interesting and by no means unoriginal theory of morality.[6]

---

[3] John Stuart Mill, "Dr. Whewell on Moral Philosophy," *Dissertations and Discussions* (2nd ed., 1867), II, p. 454. Mill's essay was originally a review of *Hist.* and *EMP*, and was published in the *Westminster Review* (October, 1852). It is the harshest and least sympathetic review Mill ever wrote.

[4] James Martineau wrote two reviews of Whewell, the first review of *EMP*, which appeared in the *Prospective Review* in 1845, the second of *LSM*, which appeared in the *Prospective Review* in 1846. Both reviews are reprinted in Martineau's *Essays, Addresses, and Reviews* (London, 1891), Vol. III, from which all quotations of Martineau will be taken.

[5] There have been some recent studies of Whewell's philosophy of science: those to which I am indebted are: C. J. Ducasse, "Whewell's Philosophy of Scientific Discovery," *The Philosophical Review*, vol. 60 (1951), reprinted in *Theories of Scientific Method*, R. M. Blake, C. J. Ducasse, and E. H. Madden, (eds.) (Seattle, 1960); and Robert E. Butts, "Necessary Truth in Whewell's Theory of Science," *American Philosophical Quarterly*, vol. 2 (1965).

[6] A thorough study of Whewell's ethics would have to include consideration not only of his acknowledged debts to Butler—these are discussed very briefly below—but those to Kant as well. The general direction of his moral thought is Kantian in its emphasis on action in accordance with rules, and in Kant's *Idea of a Universal History*, especially in the Fourth and Fifth Propositions, there are remarks which suggest almost the whole of the developmental aspect of Whewell's system. Cf. also D. Forbes, *The Liberal Anglican Idea of History* (Cambridge, 1952), especially ch. III.

I

It is only to be expected that so historically minded a thinker as Whewell should have a definite conception of the place of his own work in the development of ethics. In Whewell's case this is a matter of more than egoistic interest. The historical development of morality as well as of moral theory is central to his thought. His view of his position in the evolution of moral theory becomes clear from remarks in his *Lectures on the History of Moral Philosophy in England*. He traces English moral philosophy back, not to the casuists of the Catholic Church who gave detailed moral advice without giving detailed reasons to back it up, but to those English casuists who attempted to write books of cases for a Reformed England. These men, and especially Jeremy Taylor, discussed cases primarily as illustrations of the rules and principles which were their main concern: in this they took a step in the direction of systemizing morality.[7] The next development came as a result of the challenge Hobbes delivered to the whole traditional Christian mode of viewing morality. The challenge could neither be ignored nor easily answered. For Hobbes' system was closely allied to the new developments in science, while his traditionally minded critics were hampered by adherence to metaphysical and methodological views derived from an outworn period of thought. In the new systems of science, Whewell says, "much was so clearly convincing, that it was impossible to resist the evidence of its truth. . . . To reconstruct moral philosophy after the ancient systems of philosophy had been shaken to their foundations by the powerful hands of Descartes and Hobbes, Bacon and Newton, was no easy task." First of all it was necessary to clear away the encumbrances of the older modes of philosophizing. But Hobbes' opponents, instead of doing this, attempted to repair the ruins of the old systems, or to "dwell in huts made of wrecks and fragments." And, Whewell adds, "such indeed has been in great measure the condition of the common structures of morals up to the present day."[8] Even those who, like Clarke (and like Locke in some of his moods), tried to construct Christian moralities modelled after mathematical systems were not truly in touch with modern developments. The views of Clarke and Locke on this point are, Whewell holds, "remnants retained by them of a philosophy then past . . . If Morality is still to be capable of demonstration—if her distinctions are really steadfast and unchangeable—we must seek some new source of just principles for our reasoning, some new basis of fixity and permanency."

[7] *Hist.*, pp. 34–35.
[8] *Ibid.*, p. 59.

Of the importance of finding such a new basis, Whewell had no doubts. He saw the history of moral philosophy not as a history of debates over the logic and epistemology of morals, but as part of the constant struggle between a religious and a secular view of life, between the forces of good and those of evil, between the possibilities of salvation and the temptations to damnation. The morality of consequences pure and unalloyed is one of the allies of worldliness. Whewell always refers to it as the "low" morality, and to the morality of "principles" or motives as "high."[9] The effect of the confusion and disorder which befell the "high" school, when it failed to take account of modern scientific developments and was forced to give way to the delusively clear and disastrously simple morality of consequences, is graphically portrayed:

> The reverence which, handed down by the tradition of ages of moral and religious teaching, had hitherto protected the accustomed forms of moral good, was gradually removed. Vice, and Crime, and Sin, ceased to be words that terrified the popular spectator. Virtue, and Goodness, and Purity, were no longer things which he looked up to with mute respect. He ventured to lay a sacrilegious hand even upon these hallowed shapes. . . . There was a scene like that which occurred when the barbarians of old broke into the Eternal City. At first . . . they were awed by the divine aspect of the ancient rulers and magistrates: but when once their leader had smitten one of these venerable figures with impunity, the coarse and violent mob rushed onwards, and exultingly mingled all in one common destruction.[10]

If we find it hard to believe that philosophical theories of morality could have such devastating potentialities, Whewell—agreeing on this point at least with J. S. Mill—did not. Where Mill held that without a new and more comprehensive version of utilitarianism than Bentham had given, society would be threatened with disintegration,[11] Whewell believed that there was an urgent need for a defense of the high morality which would enable its adherents to withstand the most recent onslaughts of that low but insidious danger to men's best and truest hopes.

No existing version of the high view, Whewell held, would be adequate to the task. Bishop Butler's philosophy was the best that had been produced, but it was altogether too vague to be satisfactory any longer. Butler proved, according to Whewell, the reality of "the office" of the moral faculty. He showed that morality could be based on principles of a unique sort and could not be based on

[9] *Ibid.*, pp. 98–99.
[10] *Ibid.*, p. 101.
[11] See J. B. Schneewind's "Introduction" to his edition of *Mill's Ethical Writings* (New York, 1965), especially pp. 13–15.

calculation of consequences. But he left the exact nature and the limits of the moral faculty in doubt.[12] As a result, his achievement could easily be challenged by those who, like the utilitarians, claimed to have scientifically precise results. Butler's vagueness is what one should expect, considering where he stood in the growth of moral thought. He was doing "that which . . . discoverers always have to do. They search at the same time for true propositions and for precise definitions," each being dependent on the other.[13] As the important conceptions become clearer, the propositions involving them become more certain. "All truths are seen dimly before they are seen clearly; are conveyed in a vague and confused shape before they are expressed in a definite and lucid form."[14] If Cumberland had been the Kepler of the high morality, Butler was its Borelli or its Huyghens:[15] the inference is not far to seek that its Newton was to come.

Whewell takes this apparently fanciful parallel with science quite seriously. He thinks moral theory may be expected to develop in the way the science of mechanics did. The law of least action is the foundation of that science. But the less general and less basic principles of mechanics were not demonstrated by first discovering the law of least action and then deducing the other laws from it. Knowledge of mechanics advanced, Whewell says, by considering first of all "special problems, reasoned upon by means of principles which, in those narrower applications at least, were self-evident." As men came to have a firmer grasp on these principles, they came also to see that they were but limited cases of more general principles, "which were true because they included the partial truths at first discovered" but which were applicable far more generally. Universal principles, covering all cases, are arrived at last of all, and they never, Whewell says, become "the best mode of obtaining practical results."[16] "Now so far as this general description goes," Whewell continues, "I do not think it at all extravagant to expect that the history of the Science of Mechanics may be a type of the genuine course of real progress in other sciences, even in those which deal with the internal world of thought and feeling"—e.g., the theory of morals.[17]

[12] *Hist.*, pp. 128–129. [13] *Ibid.*, p. 132.
[14] *Ibid.*, p. 128. [15] *Ibid.*, p. 132.
[16] *Ibid.*, pp. 188–189.
[17] *Ibid.*, p. 189; and, for the identification of "internal" with "moral," see *LSM*, pp. 46–48, and *EMP*, para 68. It is worth comparing this passage with Sidgwick's "Establishment of Ethical First Principles," *Mind* (O.S.) vol. 4 (1879), in which a method very similar to this is outlined as one possible way of proving ethical first principles. Whether Sidgwick thought he himself used the method is unclear.

The idea of the development of knowledge is in fact as central to Whewell's ethics as it is to his philosophy of science (and it is significant that neither Martineau nor Mill mentions it). Both (i) Whewell's theory of the proper order for the study of morality and (ii) his understanding of the role of intuition in ethics depend on the way in which he understands the progress of knowledge. I shall indicate very briefly his views on these two points here, for this will help us to understand more fully his view of his own position *vis-à-vis* the history of ethics.

(i) On Whewell's view there are three levels at which an understanding of morality may exist. The lowest is that at which one can make moral judgments on particular cases, but cannot do much more. The next level is the level of systematic morality. Here the moral knowledge of the previous level is made more explicit and is drawn together, by means of expressly articulated rules and principles, to form a coherent whole. At the third level we come for the first time to distinctively philosophical issues. The philosopher raises questions about the sort of justification moral principles can have, the nature of moral judgments, the meaning of moral terms, the kind of reasoning needed to support detailed rules or maxims, and the relations of moral knowledge to other sorts of knowledge. Now just as a philosophy of geometry presupposes a developed system of geometry, so the (third-level) philosophy of morality presupposes a developed (second-level) system of morality; and this in turn presupposes a fairly extensive set of (first-level) particular judgments. Whewell's *Elements of Morality including Polity* was meant primarily to present a detailed system of morality on the second level. As a matter of fact it contains some passages of what strictly speaking should have been kept for a work on the philosophy of morality. But it is misunderstood if it is taken as offering answers to all of the questions which philosophers rightly pose in distinctively philosophical works.

(ii) Our knowledge of morality is progressive not only in the sense that it becomes more and more systematic and explicit, but in the sense that its contents change, for the better: we discover more and more moral truths. Discoveries of particular moral truths affect and are affected by discoveries of general principles. As we come to know more of the details, our grasp of principles increases, and as we increase our grasp of the general principles and see more clearly their self-evidence, we are increasingly able to extend their application to new cases. Consequently in morality, as in science, our understanding of the fundamental axioms or principles on which the subordinate principles rest is progressive. Since it is these axioms which we know by intuition, it must be admitted that our intuitions at any given moment are incomplete, that they contain error, and that our understanding of them is open to correction. There is a self-evident *element* involved in any moral principle, but we, or our society, may not yet have developed far enough to have grasped the self-evident element in all its clarity and fullness.

Whewell's aim, then, was to systematize the "high" morality in terms that would be defensible in an age of science. Considering inquiry as a co-operative venture, he thought of himself as continuing the work of Cudworth, Clarke, and (especially) Butler, but as bringing it into closer connection with methods derived from study of the most highly developed areas of knowledge. He thought this an important task because he thought it quite possible that the lessons taught by the higher morality might well be lost, with disastrous effects on men's well-being, here and hereafter. But he did not wish to claim any sort of finality for his own system: he saw it as at best a step in the endless progress of improvement.

II

It is easy to misunderstand Whewell when he speaks of systematizing our common moral beliefs. Indeed his own account of his procedure is most misleading. The language he uses constantly suggests that the system will be deductive on a Euclidean model. In the Preface to the first edition of the *Elements* (omitted in later editions) the comparison is explicitly drawn. Geometry proves conclusions by arguing deductively from axioms and definitions while the philosophy of geometry asks questions concerning the cogency of such proofs and the status of the axioms. In the present volume, Whewell says, he will try to construct a reasoned system of morality, since this is a prerequisite for a philosophy of morality. In the system the basic principles, of Justice, Truth, Humanity, and so on, will be "in some measure, analogous, in Morality, to the *Axioms* in Geometry."[18] And if we pay attention only to what Whewell says about the rules and principles of morality, we may well think the qualification here —"in some measure"—unnecessary.

The construction of a system of morality presupposes three propositions, on Whewell's view: (a) that "there are moral truths," (b) that "moral truths ought to be expressed in a permanent and definite

[18] *EMP*, 1st ed. (1845), Preface; and see *LSM*, p. 43.

form," and (c) that "such moral truths are rationally connected one with another;—that one moral truth depends upon another, in a manner which we can apprehend by our reason, express by reasoning."[19] The first proposition may be proven by appeal to instances, i.e., by appeal to clear cases of moral truths, such as the principles that we ought in general to obey the laws of our country and that the laws of our country ought to be just. Like all nineteenth-century English moral philosophers, Whewell has no doubts on this point. He is not interested in controverting moral scepticism. The second proposition is a general requirement of reason wherever truth is concerned. The third point is also a general requirement of reason. But it is in addition true by definition of *moral* truths. Whatever feelings we may have, Whewell says, they do not count as moral unless they are rational: "feeling is not moral feeling if it excludes the operation of the human faculty, the Reason." Not even the dictates of conscience are morally authoritative unless they are warranted by Reason. "The true guide of man is Conscience, only so long as the guide of Conscience is Reason,"[20] Whewell says, and he claims that moralists of all ages, as well as the plain man, would agree. The present-day systematizer of morality, then, is to take the implicit moral knowledge of mankind and make it explicit.[21] He has not to invent new duties, to deny established rights, or to find new reasons for moral judgments: he has only to work the judgments of common sense into "a Body of Moral Truths, definitely expressed and rationally connected," and to arrange the reasons for these truths in a rational and connected manner.[22] The first step in doing this is to define the central terms of morality. These definitions have to be "reciprocal," i.e., we must explain the meaning of one moral term by using another. And we must take it for granted that the ordinary meaning of the terms is already known, otherwise there will be no way to explain their meaning.[23] We must then go on to discover the assumptions involved in our use of these terms, for the assumptions will figure among the principles of morality. But it is the search for *first* principles which is the major task of the systematizer. We know that there must be such first principles, because we know that morality is rational. The argument Whewell has in mind here is the familiar one, that without a first principle, or set of first principles,

---

[19] *LSM*, pp. 10–17.
[20] *Ibid.*, p. 19; cf. pp. 143–147. See Sidgwick on this point, *Methods of Ethics*, Book I, Chapter III, Sect. 1.
[21] *LSM*, p. 20.
[22] *Ibid.*, and cf., pp. 75–76.
[23] *Ibid.*, pp. 26–27.

there would be a vicious infinite regress in reasons for subordinate principles or rules. "We must," he says,

> by going backwards from point to point, at length arrive at some *First Principles*, from which the whole reasoning proceeds. . . . there must be, in Morality, Axioms and Postulate . . . if our system is to be a body of Moral Truths presented according to their rational connection.[24]

These first principles must be intuitively evident. For it must be possible to know that they are true, and yet "we do not and cannot deduce them, in their full evidence and extent, from any more fundamental principles of which they are the consequences and applications."[25]

After this it is scarcely surprising to find that Martineau took Whewell to be trying to construct a geometrical morality. It may be helpful to note the criticisms Martineau directs at the analogy Whewell draws and to see what replies Whewell would make. Martineau objects to the comparison of geometry and morality because "morality is not, like geometry, a *science*, but an *art*," and the order called for in a treatise on an art is the practical order, not the logical order demanded in a treatise on a science. Hence, Martineau argues, if Whewell has presented us with a deductive system, it cannot be a system of morality; and if he has given us a system of morality it cannot be deductive.[26] A further point is involved here. The language of art is imperative, Martineau claims, and the rules of an art are what we try to learn, to teach, and to systematize. But "precept is not deducible from precept as truth is from truth": it is absurd to suppose that "Do not kill" can be deduced from "Do not commit adultery."[27] The only place for deduction within an art is in the application of known rules to unproblematic cases. If there existed a clear and precise verbal revelation of a code of morals, then the Christian moralist could confine himself to acting as a judge and deciding the application of the code to cases. This seems to be how Whewell views morality, Martineau says, and it is one of his major shortcomings, for he does not realize that the moralist, like the legislator, must "shape into language a code yet unformed."[28]

To this criticism there are four things to be said, which may help

---

[24] *Ibid.*, pp. 32–33; and cf. *EMP*, para. 73.
[25] *EMP*, 2nd ed. (1848), Preface.
[26] Martineau, *op. cit.*, p. 372. I give only page references, since the distinction between the two reviews is unimportant.
[27] *Ibid.*, p. 385.
[28] *Ibid.*, p. 386. The last point seems to be a particularly absurd criticism to direct against Whewell.

both to turn whatever force it possesses and, more importantly, to clarify Whewell's position. (a) Whewell agrees with Martineau on the imperatival status of moral judgments. "The natural utterance of Morality is commands. Her declarations are Rules."[29] (b) Despite this he holds that there is truth and falsity in the moral realm. The material sciences dealing with the "outer" world enable us to discover the laws of what *is*, while the sciences dealing with the "inner" realm give us laws of what *ought to be*. "The true method," Whewell says, "in each course, must lead . . . to a System of Truths; but the very nature of the Truth appears to differ in the one system and in the other."[30] Unfortunately Whewell does not explain the kind of truth that moral imperatives can have. But it seems as if he held that such imperatives can have a proper truth of their own and not merely a justifiability borrowed from the truth of related declaratives in the relevant science, which is the view Martineau upholds, here following Mill. (c) If this is Whewell's view, then one can see one possible justification for his claim that there must be rational connections among moral truths themselves, not only in factual propositions which serve as their grounds. (Here again Whewell is silent, but these questions presumably belong to moral philosophy, not to the task of systematizing morality.) (d) The rational connection among moral truths need not, however, be of the simple straight-line deductive sort which Martineau—quite understandably misled by Whewell's presentation—criticizes. Whewell does not in fact claim to intuit a single basic principle nor even a small set of basic axioms, and then go on to derive further detailed rules of action. As we might expect from the comparison he draws between the science of mechanics and moral philosophy, his procedure is quite different. He uses two considerations for the systematization of morality: that there must be one supreme rule of morality, and that this rule must be a rule for human beings.

(i) There must be one supreme rule of morality because otherwise morality could not be rational. It may be objected, as Martineau objected to a similar claim concerning the Highest Good,[31] that the argument so far given (as summarized and quoted above) shows at best that there must be some unproven principles but not that there can be only one such principle. To this Whewell's reply is as follows. A supreme rule must do four things: cover all actions of individuals,

---

[29] *LSM*, p. 46; *EMP*, para. 16.
[30] *LSM*, pp. 45, 48. The same point is made in the later lectures: see *Hist. Add.*, pp. 112 ff. where some interesting arguments are suggested: and *Hist. Add.*, p. 128.
[31] Martineau, *op. cit.*, p. 360.

govern all spheres of life, adjudicate the disputes between the spheres of life, and assign men's possessions in each sphere.[32] A supreme rule must therefore be such that it can do these things. Hence it is plausible to argue that there can be only one such rule. For if there were more than one, they might come into conflict and there would be no rational way to settle the conflict. And then morality would not be fully rational. Thus the demand that morality be rational does in the end lead to the position that there can be only one supreme moral principle.[33] But despite Mill's sarcasms on this point,[34] Whewell does not attempt to obtain the actual content of the supreme rule from this argument alone.

(ii) The supreme rule must be a rule for human beings. No argument is given for this, but the point is plain: we are systematizing morality insofar as it applies to humans. We know that there are some moral truths, and we know what some of them are. The force of the present consideration is to raise the question of the conditions under which human beings can live in accordance with a supreme moral rule. It is through this formulation of the problem that human nature becomes the determining factor in Whewell's systematization of morality. For although in its finished form a systematization of morality may look like a Euclidean system, the details of the system are to be derived by a consideration of the needs which arise from the demand that men, with their actual passions and desires, live a life guided by a supreme moral rule. Whewell frequently, and confusingly, speaks as if his method of systematizing morality were a method of *discovering* moral rules. But at his best he is clear that this is not its primary function. We start, as at a certain point the science of mechanics started, with a large number of acknowledged truths. By viewing them in the twin lights of the necessity for a supreme rule and the facts of human nature, we can systematize these truths. And we can, with the system, then advance to further knowledge. Making allowance for Whewell's somewhat misleading use of the term "determining," his statement to Herschel is as compact and clear as anything he said on the matter:

---

[32] *LSM*, pp. 80–81.

[33] It is not clear how this demand for rationality in a moral system is to be reconciled with some of Whewell's other views, such as those on cases of necessity (see Sect. VIII below). The view of rationality which Whewell uses here is similar to the view adopted by Bentham and Mill, but the later view is closer to Bradley's: cf. *Ethical Studies* (1876), 2nd ed. (Oxford, 1935), pp. 193–199, and the even more vehement attacks on casuistry in the *Principles of Logic* (1922), 2nd ed. (Oxford, 1950), pp. 269–271.

[34] Mill, *op. cit.*, pp. 491–493.

I cannot find any way of determining Moral Rules by considering them as means of getting some external object. I do find the means of determining such Rules by looking at the constitution of man . . . I found my Morality, not upon something which man is to get, but on something which he is to *be*. He is to be truly a *man*: he is to conform to Rules . . . *moral* Rules . . . We must conceive that man *is* a moral being, and then try to see *how* he can be so.

I do not reject *experience*; for it is by experience that we become acquainted with man's constitution . . . Experience enables me to understand man's constitution more and more clearly, so that I can see how he may be, and may be made, moral.[35]

Existing morality, in other words, is to be viewed as the result of a continuing effort to solve the problem: how is a being with a human nature to live under the guidance of a supreme moral rule? Whewell's systematization of morality is an attempt to articulate the contents of morality as a reasoned answer to this question. The intuited first principle(s) will be seen as bringing order into the moral knowledge we already have.[36]

III

Whewell's view of the function of the concepts of a supreme rule and of human nature can be further explained in terms of his general theory of the knowledge. Every science, he holds, has relevant to it and is demarcated by, certain distinctive Ideas or Conceptions. Mechanics involves the Idea of Force, Chemistry that of Elementary Composition, Physiology that of Vital Powers. And "each science must advance by means of its *appropriate* Conceptions," i.e., one cannot use conceptions drawn from mechanics to explain chemistry, nor conceptions drawn from chemistry to explain physiology.[37] Now the Idea of an area of investigation bears a special relation to the basic axioms which hold true within that area. The axioms are elementary truths, not true by definition, but necessarily true nonetheless. They are therefore self-evident necessary truths and as such can be called "intuitive." But it is a result of the limited powers of the human mind that what is self-evident in itself may not be immediately self-evident to us, nor be seen to be necessarily true by all men at all times. "Truths may be self-evident when we have made a certain progress in thinking, which are not self-evident when we begin to think," because the mind needs to develop.[38] There are

---

[35] Letter of July 3, 1846, in Todhunter, *op. cit.*, vol. II, p. 338.
[36] *LSM*, p. 137.
[37] *Novum Organon Renovatum* (London, 3rd edition, 1858), p. 42.
[38] *LSM*, p. 38.

axioms, "tactily assumed or occasionally stated," which "belong to all the Ideas which form the foundations of the sciences, and are constantly employed in the reasoning and speculations of those who think clearly on such subjects."[39] The axioms may even be articulated before their necessity is clearly realized. That we may see the necessity of the axioms, we must have attained clarity about the fundamental Idea of the science. Considering the axioms as rules to which our thinking must conform if we are to reach truth in a given science, Whewell says: "In order . . . that we may see the necessary cogency of these rules we must possess, clearly and steadily, the Ideas from which the rules flow"[40]—e.g., in order to understand the proof of the axiom of composition of forces, we must have the Idea of Cause "molded into a distinct Conception of Statical Force." Thus the axioms "flow from" the basic Idea of a discipline when that Idea has been given sufficient clarity. And Whewell then tells us that the criterion of having reached sufficient clarity is "that the person shall *see* the necessity of the Axioms belonging to each Idea;—shall accept them in such a manner as to perceive the cogency of the reasonings founded upon them."[41] For instance, one has a clear idea of space if one follows geometrical proofs and sees that they are conclusive.

Now the development of an Idea into clarity is not a self-evolvement in the Hegelian manner. It is a result of the attempt to understand the area in which the Idea is fundamental, of an attempt, that is, to organize the Facts in terms of the Idea. We use our implicit apprehension of an Idea to organize some of the facts which we have observed; the observations in turn, organized in this manner, show us further aspects of the Idea, and help us to a more explicit awareness of it, and this, again leads us to further observations, reorganization, etc. On Whewell's view all knowledge results from this sort of interplay between Idea and Fact, between theory and observation. Moral knowledge, though different in kind from scientific knowledge, yet displays the same fundamental pattern of growth. The Idea, for morality, is the Idea of a Supreme Rule. The Facts are the Facts of Human Nature. Moral philosophy is the investigation of human nature conceived as being under a supreme rule; or it is the investigation of a supreme rule as applied to beings with a human nature. We may begin with a brief review of the Facts.

[39] *Novum Organon Renovatum, op. cit.*, p. 41.
[40] *Loc. cit.*
[41] *Ibid.*, p. 42.

IV

There are two elements in human nature to which Whewell devotes little comment: reason and will. Obviously both are important—reason is what is distinctive about the human animal; will is what makes us active and hence in need of a morality in the first place—but Whewell has nothing new to say about either. Reason shows itself in our ability to do more than simply have sensations of particulars. It is essentially tied to operations with ideas, or to working with generalizations and universals. It enables us to group our sensations into classes, to form abstractions, to discover general laws, to unite these laws into theories, to perform various kinds of inferences, and to "apprehend fundamental principles," i.e., to grasp self-evident truths.[42] Whewell sometimes speaks of reason as a "faculty," but the locution is merely a convenience, since by "faculty" he means only "class of operations."[43] He is even more taciturn about will: "Will, or Volition, is the last step of intention, the first step of action. It is the internal act which leads to external acts." An external act is said to be mine if it proceeds from my will, and I am free when acts proceed from my will, but not otherwise. The will itself, Whewell says, "is stimulated to action by certain Springs of Action,"[44] and that, in effect, is the whole of his account of will. He does not discuss the issue of freedom of the will anywhere, so far as I have been able to discover, and the few further references to will in the *Elements* do not suffice to inform us of his views, although the mechanistic imagery he occasionally uses[45] suggests that he may have held a determinist view. In any event it is the Springs of Action which are his main psychological interest.

Whewell divides the motivating forces which "stimulate" the human will into five classes: appetites, affections, mental desires, moral sentiments, and reflex sentiments. He views the classification as an advance along the lines Butler laid out. The first two classes[46] correspond to Butler's direct desires and particular passions; the "appetites," including the natural cravings, are directed toward things, and the "affections" are directed toward persons and involve feelings, not simply cravings. The last two classes of springs of action

---

[42] *EMP*, paras. 2–11.
[43] *LSM*, p. 29; cf. *EMP*, para. 65.
[44] *EMP*, paras. 15, 24; cf. 61, where he says that motives do not act on the will as forces act on bodies, but does not say how they *do* act.
[45] See, e.g., *EMP*, para. 78.
[46] *Ibid.*, paras. 26–33.

analyze what Butler called, comprehensively, "conscience." Whewell does not make any use of the idea of a separate faculty whose sole function is to pass moral judgments. He attributes that task to reason. But he sees the need for some account of the moral feelings and of the phenomenology of conscience and attempts to give it in his discussion of these two types of spring of action. The moral sentiments are directed first at actions and later—in individual as well as in social development—at persons. They are dependent on prior judgments, not simply on conceptions, and include indignation, resentment, approval, disapproval, and esteem, all of which presuppose a sense of rightness or wrongness, goodness or badness.[47] The reflex sentiments are directed toward other judgments and sentiments concerning ourselves. Among them are the desire of being loved and the desire of being esteemed, which involve the judgments of other men about us, desire of our own approval, and the feelings of self-admiration.[48] It is in the class of mental desires, which replace Butler's cool self-love and calm benevolence, that Whewell sees the most important springs of action for morality. These springs result in part from the fact that the objects of human desire tend to present themselves to the mind in the form of abstract conceptions (because man is a reasonable being). Another part of the class is comprised of those desires which could not exist in any form without abstract conceptions and without the operations of memory and imagination projecting remembered goods and evils into the future and thus giving rise to hope and fear.[49] There are numerous mental desires. Whewell gives a rough classification of them, which he does not take to be exhaustive but which includes those most important for his purpose. They are as follows. (a) The desire of safety. Whewell considers this, rather than the more general desire of personal well-being which, he says, could be taken as a sort of summary of all the appetites and affections, because we need something more definite and limited in order to "frame rules of action." The desire of safety reflects a minimal need of all men: without safety, life is not tolerable at all. Hence it is a strong and universal desire. This desire expands, in man, to include not only life and security, but ease, comfort, tranquility, and other aims of the same sort. Whewell takes it to include also the desire of absence of restraint on one's actions, or Liberty.[50] (b) The desire of having. Whewell thinks that even in some

[47] *Ibid.*, para. 56.
[48] *Ibid.*, paras. 57–60.
[49] *Ibid.*, paras. 35–37.
[50] *Ibid.*, paras. 39–42.

animals there is a desire for possessions which extends beyond a desire for simple means of subsistence. In man this desire is extremely strong. It is the source of all the struggles over property in things, but it is diversified by the other appetites and affections, which demand possessions for their satisfaction. Whewell adds, interestingly, that "without Property, and the recognition of Property in Society, even man's free agency cannot exist." Action requires means of actions, and freedom of action requires security in the disposal of such means.[51] (c) The desire of society. Whewell considers this to have two forms, one a desire of family society, the other a desire of civil society. The latter is connected but not identical with (d) the need of a mutual understanding among men. This need is the general form of the need that shows itself not only in promise making, but also in the division of labor and the assignment of various jobs, positions, offices, etc. Whewell speaks of a need rather than a desire here to emphasize the urgency of having mutual understanding: without it, the whole community "would crumble into dust."[52] (e) The desire of Superiority. Whewell holds that while it is obviously impossible for this desire to be satisfied in all men, it can lead to a situation in which something desirable is obtained. For it can lead to a system of equal rules for the protection of whatever a man has, by transformation into a refusal to be inferior, which can work out into an acceptance of equality.[53] Whewell finally mentions (f) the desire of knowledge, which shows itself at first in simple curiosity, but has a far greater importance than that. It is the same as the mind's desire to grow and develop, and it transforms other objects of desire in numerous ways, and is thereby the means by which reason influences action. In fact, "our knowledge, thus considered as a Spring of Action, is identical with the Reason, by which we contemplate abstract and general conceptions, and thus determine for ourselves rules and ends of action."[54]

These then are the Facts of Human Nature which we are to view in the light of the Idea of a Supreme Moral Rule. The Facts could of course be investigated for their own sake, as the science of psychology would investigate them. As this science progresses, our understanding of the Facts may well alter in ways that affect the way we systematize morality. This is one of the reasons why Whewell's system can make no claim to finality.

[51] *Ibid.*, paras. 45–46.
[52] *Ibid.*, paras. 47–52.
[53] *Ibid.*, paras. 52–53.
[54] *Ibid.*, paras. 54–55.

V

Whewell's systemization of rational reconstruction of ordinary morality involves the continual use of two basic ideas. One is that there is a permanent moral demand on men. The other is that there is a real historical development of morality in response to this demand. The existing morality of a group at any time is to be seen as the outcome of the permanent demand working on and in human nature, under certain circumstances of environment and history. I begin with the permanent factor.

Reason, as we have seen, is the distinctive part of man. This is shown, from the side of the facts, by our tendency to identify ourselves with our reason rather than with our passions or appetites.[55] It is shown on the side of conception in our necessarily thinking of man as rational. Now since reason is the distinctive part of man, Whewell says that "Man acts as man, when he acts under the influence of reason."[56] The permanent demand in human beings is simply that they act *as men*. The facts of human nature make it inevitable that men will act to satisfy their desires, and Whewell has no hesitation in pointing out that, unless they could do so, life would be intolerable. But the gratification of desires, the satisfaction of appetites, and the expression of passions are not distinctively human unless they are in accordance with the demands of reason. What does this mean?

The distinctively human modes of action are all *rule-involving* modes of action. "Reason directs us to Rules," Whewell says, and the ground of the assertion is that Reason is the generalizing faculty. In connection with action, generalizations are rules. "Rules of action are necessary, therefore, for the action of man as man. We cannot conceive man as man, without conceiving him as subject to Rules, and making part of an Order in which Rules prevail."[57] As we should expect this claim is in part a factual claim. Wives are not just biological mates, and children not just offspring; property is more than brute possession, a society more than a crowd of people. The distinctively human element in family, property, and society is rule-defined activity—and rules presuppose reason. Thus as a matter of fact when we think of men as men, as distinctively human, we are thinking of them as living lives in which rule-directed action is essential. But the claim is more than simply factual,

---
[55] *Ibid.*, para. 63.
[56] *Ibid.*, para. 67.
[57] *Ibid.*

because the demands of reason are not identical with demands for conformity to existing rules. Reason by itself is "authoritative": following Butler, Whewell takes this to be self-evident. "We cannot help recognizing, in the Reason, an authority to repress and resist Appetite and Desire, when the two come into conflict." Reason is an inner light whose function is to guide us.[58] Its permanent demand is that we act in terms of rules. Only when and as we do so are we acting as human beings. The question that arises is: how *can* beings with our passional and self-centered nature act in terms of rules? The answer is to be found by examining the historical growth of morality and of our understanding of it.

VI

The guiding idea in Whewell's view of the development of morality is that mankind progresses from a state of grudging external obedience to a set of laws making social life tolerable toward a state of inner obedience and the desire to be virtuous in character, and then, at least in some instances, on to a state of sanctification of moral obedience through religious submission to the will of God. Different parts of our morality are to be understood as resulting from, and serving the varying purposes of, those different stages of man's growth toward a fully human existence. Whewell does not think that the earlier stages are abandoned as mankind progresses. There are permanent aspects of human nature to which the earlier parts of the development of morality were responses, and consequently these aspects of morality remain even at the later stages, though they are then given a subordinate place. We may outline some of the steps of the development, beginning, as Whewell does, with Rights.

First, "right" as an adjective is said to mean simply "conformable to rule." If the rule involved is a rule laid down as means to some end, the rightness is relative; if the rule involved is the Supreme Rule, then the rightness is absolute.[59] Next Whewell proceeds to give the following complex explanation of the concept of a Right (in accordance with his practice I shall capitalize the substantive term but not the adjective). (a) Rules are to guide our actions with regard to the main objects of desire and needs, and therefore rules must be framed in terms of the abstractions which refer to those objects. (b) These rules will sometimes dictate actions which would go against

[58] *Ibid.*, para. 68.
[59] *Ibid.*, paras. 71–73.

the agent's own interests and desires. (c) Hence if the rules are to be obeyed, there must be a motive countering the motive derived from the natural spring of action which will be thwarted, to lead the agent to follow the rule. (d) These counterbalancing motives can only exist, Whewell thinks, if the abstractions in terms of which the rules are framed are "realized among men," i.e., if there actually are wives, property, contracts, security, etc. And finally, (e) the rules must be subordinate to the Supreme Rule of Morality, or more precisely, they must be *moral* rules. Whewell gives no explanation of this puzzling requirement, and it seems to be question-begging. He may, however, mean that the demand of morality is (as Kant would have it) always for strict universality, and that this tends toward the elimination of partiality in the rules and in their application. If this is his meaning, he is at least not guilty of circular argument, because he takes Reason to be the faculty of generalizing or forming rules and he is here beginning the derivation of morality from the demands of Reason acting on human passions. From all this, at any rate, Whewell concludes with an explication of the concept of Rights: "Abstractions, vested in particular Persons, as possessions, by Rules subordinate to the Supreme Rule, are Rights."[60] The point, I take it, is that if men are to act as men—and morality requires that they do so—they must act according to rules, and the rules must be truly universal ("subordinate to the Supreme Rule"). To act according to such rules, they must have motives to do so, motives which will counterbalance the force of the natural springs of action. A general system of protection of each man's possessions will give everyone such counterbalancing motives (and presumably nothing else will). Therefore in order that men may be in a position to act as men, such possessions ought to be protected: "in order that Moral Rules may exist, Men must have Rights."[61] For example, everyone desires personal safety. Left to himself, each person would, out of fear and apprehension, tend to be belligerent and aggressive. But where a positive Right to safety is established, no one will need to worry about attacks from others, each may be calm and secure, and "in this calm, man . . . can act with a reference to Rules founded on other Men's Rights; and can thus, and not otherwise, exercise his rational and moral nature."[62]

The derivation of the principal Rights relies directly on Whewell's analysis of the springs of action. Taking it that the mental desires are

[60] *Ibid.*, para. 78.
[61] *Ibid.*
[62] *Ibid.*, para. 79.

the major desires, since, among other things, they sum up, in humans, the appetites and affections, Whewell argues that corresponding to each major mental desire—the desire for safety, for possession, for family society, for civil society, and for mutual understanding and reliance—there must be a Right: the Rights of personal security, of property, of contract, of family, and of government. Whewell allows that other mental desires, as well as other springs of action, may require the establishment of Rights, but these are the five "primary, and universal" Rights.[63]

The establishment of Rights serves another purpose in addition to that already noted. It is the first step toward genuine morality. Living in a society where Rights are established, men develop a feeling of attachment to those Rights. We are first attached to our own Rights, since they secure us in possession of various goods, but this sentiment tends to grow into "an affection for Rights in general"[64] and into a resentment of violations of Rights, whether ours or another's. These "jural sentiments," as Whewell calls them (for the Rights around which the feelings grow are so far only positive legal or customary Rights), "are the germs of Moral sentiments." We come to appreciate not only actions in accordance with Rights, but the dispositions that lead men to act so, and to condemn not only violations of Rights but the dispositions which lead to them.[65] And this begins to be properly a moral feeling, because morality, Whewell says, is concerned with the inner side of action, with intentions, motives, and dispositions. Other aspects of morality grow from this starting point. We need not follow all the details of the development from law to morality, but some are essential to see how Whewell completes the transition from the bare statement that there must be a supreme rule which is appropriate for human beings to the contents of that rule.

We have already noted Whewell's account of the term "right" in general. Some of his remaining terminology, which is remarkable chiefly for its ineptitude, must now be explained. Whewell makes the term "obligation" correlative to "Rights," thus deliberately narrowing its ordinary use. Where someone has a Right others have obligations to respect his possessions. To "right" there corresponds "duty," i.e., if an act is right for me to do, then it is my duty. "Duty" is accordingly, Whewell says, a wider term than "obligation," just as "right" is a wider term than "Right." We can be obliged to

---

[63] *Ibid.*, paras. 79–80.
[64] *Ibid.*, para. 98.
[65] *Ibid.*, para. 101.

carry out our obligations to those who have Rights. There is no corresponding notion for duty, although we may say that those who would be benefited by our doing of our duty have a moral claim on us. Duties are actions considered as being right, virtues are "habits of soul by which we perform duties," and vices are habitual transgressions of duties.[66] These points are worth noting if only because a clear grasp of them makes it obvious that at least two of Mill's accusations concerning "vicious circles" are quite mistaken, as Whewell himself pointed out forcefully in an Appendix to a later edition of the *Elements*.[67]

Morality, for Whewell as for all other English intuitionists during the nineteenth century, is not primarily a matter of overt action but rather of inner action-producing states: desire, will, intention, motive. Whewell holds that such inner states "point to external Acts," and in what seems at first a very Benthamite statement, he says that they derive their moral significance "from the external Acts to which they thus point." If the acts to which, e.g., the desire of having points are wrong, then the desire itself is wrong. But we are to distinguish between laws, which express rules of overt action, and "moral precepts," which state rules for inner states. Where the law is "Do not steal," the moral precept is "Do not covet." With some confusion of terminology, Whewell now says that "Moral Precepts express our Duties," and allows a variety of ways of stating such precepts, using the locutions "It is wrong to . . .," "We ought not to . . .," "We must not . . .," "We should not . . .," and others.[68] Now the original wrongness or rightness of overt acts arises from positive law, and since the moral character of inner act-producing states is derived from the character of the overt acts to which they lead, there is a sense in which morality is based on law. This aspect of Whewell's system is carried out in his use of the classification of Rights as the basis for the classification of moral precepts and duties. There is at least one moral precept corresponding to each class of positive Rights. Whewell states them as follows: Be not angry, bear no malice (corresponding to Rights of the Person); Do not covet (corresponding to Rights of property); Do not lie, do not deceive (corresponding to Rights of contract and promise-making); Do not lust (corresponding to Rights of society).[69] But the correspondence with legal rights is only the start of morality, not its completion.

[66] *Ibid.*, paras. 75–94.
[67] Mill, *op. cit.*, pp. 486 ff. *EMP*, Appendix, ch. II, paras. 1–5.
[68] *EMP*, paras. 106–109.
[69] *Ibid.*, para. 110.

It will be noted that the precepts so far stated are all prohibitive. Morality in its fuller development gives positive commandments.

VII

The connection between the positive and negative aspects of morality, and the transcendence of merely legal morality, is made through the idea of moral goodness. When we think of the dispositions enjoined by the moral precepts as all connected together in a personality, we have the beginnings of the Idea of moral goodness or virtue. And as we consider the Idea of a supreme rule of action in connection with these dispositions, our idea of moral goodness becomes increasingly clear. We see that all actions (and not just those specified by positive Rights and Obligations) ought to be regulated by virtuous dispositions, and that all inner act-producing states ought to be "formed by Virtue and Duty," so that the whole man is shaped by the idea of moral goodness. Considering this point further we see that because there are separate desires in men the idea of moral goodness involves the idea of a set of separate virtues. And because "any special Virtue implies a Class of Duties; and a Class of Duties may be enjoined by a Precept . . . the separate Virtues . . . may be represented by certain comprehensive Maxims or Principles of Duty, all of which must necessarily form portions of the Supreme Rule of Human Action."[70] These considerations contain Whewell's introduction of the concept of moral goodness or virtue as a device for systematizing our moral knowledge. The considerations rest on an appeal to the ability of each of us to make certain kinds of progress in our own thinking about morality, not simply on the theoretical usefulness of the concept. The progress of our insight corresponds to mankind's progress from an external "low" morality toward a true "high" morality.

Whewell next attempts to derive a set of highly abstract moral principles from the consideration of how the idea of moral goodness would apply to beings having a human nature. These principles will constitute the contents of the supreme rule, considered mainly from the side of the Idea. They are not as they stand specific enough to guide action: for that, further consideration of man and his society from the side of the Facts is required. The derivation of the moral principles proceeds as follows. We first specify the different virtues

[70] *Ibid.*, paras. 111–113.

into which the idea of moral goodness must be differentiated to apply to man. The derivation rests on the claim that moral goodness must belong to man as man: hence moral goodness cannot include anything divisive, anything merely selfish, for the merely private is not part of man as such; nor can it consist in simple gratification of bodily appetites, for this would not be distinctively human; nor can it consist of gratification of affections as such, for the same reason.[71] But the absence of all divisive desires and feelings may be called "Benevolence," and as such may be counted as one of the virtues. Stated as a principle of action, we may say that "Man is to be loved as Man": this is the principle of humanity. Because, again, morality excludes selfishness, and yet men are strongly acquisitive, there must be a virtue governing possession and distribution of goods, and this is Justice, the principle of which is that "each man is to have his own." Third, because men must be able to understand one another in order to live together, and must live together in order to be moral agents, there must be a virtue of Integrity or Truthfulness. Stated briefly its principle is that "we must speak the truth." Put more exactly its principle is that "we must conform our language to the universal understanding among men which the use of language implies." Fourth, because men are vexed with numerous desires, some of which are subordinate to others (this notion of subordination is not explained), we may include the virtue of Purity among the basic virtues. Its express principle is that "the Lower Parts of our Nature are to be governed by the Higher." Finally, the need of men for civil society makes imperative the inclusion of a virtue of Order among our group: its principle is that "we must accept positive Laws as the necessary conditions of Morality."[72] Benevolence, Justice, Truth, Purity, and Order, then, are the five basic virtues, the realization of which in a man's dispositions would make him a good man. They must be considered not as wholly separate, but as fusing together into a love of goodness, the attainment of which sums up the "disposition enjoined by the Supreme Law of Human Action."[73] Two additional principles are then added. The first is Earnestness: "the Affections and Intentions must not only be rightly directed, but energetic"; and the second is the principle of Moral Purpose: "things are to be sought universally . . . as means to moral ends."[74] These two "meta-principles" complete the list of basic principles. They alone

---

[71] *Ibid.*, paras. 114–116.
[72] *Ibid.*, paras. 118–122; cf. paras. 160–162.
[73] *Ibid.*, para. 129.
[74] *Ibid.*, paras. 163–164.

are not derived directly by considering man's natural desires and affections in the light of the idea of a supreme rule.

The only additional point that must be made here concerns Whewell's use of positive law in the construction of morality. Mill and Martineau were not alone in criticizing Whewell's use of it,[75] but everyone seems to have misunderstood what he was doing. Law is in no sense, for Whewell, fixed and final. As a source of morality it is at most a starting point. As the dispositions to act lawfully develop into moral virtues, and as these in turn grow into a more comprehensive attempt to attain the goodness of the good man, law will be criticized as unjust, inadequate to our understanding of morality, and in need of change. While it is true that at any given time the main bulk of the detailed duties in which the virtues are to be actualized is determined by positive law, and while it is true that there is, according to Whewell, a *prima facie* obligation to obey the laws, there is nothing in his work to rule out attempts to change the laws. Whewell puts the point succinctly in replying to Mill's attack: "Morality and Law do not depend upon each other mutually, but rather, alternately; Morality improving Law, and Law defining Morality."[76] Law lays down the details concerning property, contract, marriage rights, etc., and thus defines morality in the sense of detailing actions required by a virtuous person: Morality, giving us standards for judgment which are logically independent of the existing positive laws, gives us grounds for criticizing those laws when they lead to gross injustice, as, e.g., the slavery laws did.[77] Whewell, in taking this position, is attempting to reconcile the observed variation in positive law and morality with the validity of moral principles and with their necessary truth. His general position is that the rules of morality are "universal and immutable" so far as they flow from the Idea of morality and from human nature. The rules differ so far as they require specification by the customs and laws of the communities in which they are operative.[78] Whewell had no great admiration for Hegel,[79] but the position he develops is not far in many respects from the Hegelian position

---

[75] See, e.g., the anonymous review in *Atheneum* (July 19, 1845), pp. 709–710.
[76] *EMP*, Appendix, ch. II, para. 6.
[77] On slavery see Whewell's discussion in *EMP*, paras. 424-439.
[78] *Ibid.*, paras. 95-96 and ff.
[79] "There is nothing which so entirely deprives me of all respect for German heads in the matter of reasoning as the way in which they have allowed Hegel to domineer over them. It appears to me that on every subject he is equally fanciful and shallow . . .": Whewell to J. C. Hare (1849). From a letter given in Todhunter, *op. cit.*, Vol. II, p. 353.

regarding the relation of the universals of morality to their instantiations.

We need not follow Whewell further in the task of connecting the Idea of a Supreme Rule with the Facts of human nature and society. There are detailed chapters discussing the various specific terms for virtues and vices and showing how they fall under the main headings of virtues, other chapters dwelling on the details of our duties and showing how they are to be understood in the light of the five basic principles which together constitute the supreme rule. The opinions Whewell chooses to systematize are neither idiosyncratic nor interesting, and hence they may well be representative of the moral opinions of a large number of people. To study them as such would be a different task from ours: I hope enough has been said here to provide an understanding of Whewell's general aim and his method of accomplishing it.[80]

VIII

In various places Whewell expresses the conviction that a complete system of morality must do justice to all the widely accepted moral opinions of mankind.[81] In accordance with this conviction he attempts to find a place for the views of his chief opponents, the defenders of the ethics of consequences or the "dependent" morality, within the framework of his own "independent" morality. He is quite prepared to admit that pleasure is good and pain, in general, bad. But they are not the only things which are good or bad. Consideration of them alone will not lead us to the ideas of specifically *moral* goodness and badness, because those ideas require references to motives and dispositions and cannot involve reference only to what is logically independent of them. A dim perception of this point has led mankind always to refuse to believe that the measure of utility is the measure of morality. At the same time, no one has ever succeeded in showing how a conscience or a moral sense could be anything but vague and indefinite, and this accounts for the general dissatisfaction with views that rely on them alone. We must be able to take

---

[80] For Whewell's view on the progress from morality to religion, cf. *EMP*, paras. 460 ff. In Book III of *EMP* much of the detailed material already covered from a purely moral standpoint in Book II is treated again from the religious standpoint.

[81] *EMP*, 4th ed. (1864), Preface; *LSM*, pp. 128-129. John Grote, Whewell's successor as Knightbridge Professor, shared this view, and, as is well known, so did Sidgwick, who studied under Grote.

account of both of these points if we are to achieve an adequate systematization:

> On the one hand, the distinction of right and wrong, of moral good and evil, of virtue and vice, must be a *peculiar distinction*, different from the mere distinction of pleasure and pain, gain and loss; —on the other hand, this distinction must be one *not* immediately apprehended by any peculiar sense or faculty . . . but must be a distinction discerned by some use of the faculty of Reason which is common to all mankind.[82]

And as we must accept both the main claim of the utilitarian school (which Whewell understands to be its objection to a mysterious faculty of intuition) and the main claim of the "independent" school (the uniqueness of moral goodness) concerning the foundation, so we must reconcile their claims concerning the outcome of morality. Morality must lead to happiness. Whewell does not think we can properly support this view by arguing that production of happiness is the *criterion* of rightness. We must rather believe that action in accordance with the Supreme Rule of morality will *in fact* produce happiness for all, to the proper extent and degree.

> Since Happiness is necessarily the Supreme Object of our Desires, and Duty the Supreme Rule of our actions, there can be no harmony in our being, except our Happiness coincide with our duty. . . . As moral beings, our Happiness must be found in our Moral Progress, and in the consequences of our Moral Progress: we must be happy by being virtuous.[83]

"How this is to be," he adds, "Religion alone can fully instruct us. . . . The identification of Happiness with Duty on merely philosophical grounds is a question of great difficulty."[84]

This cheerful *rapprochement* with Utilitarianism leads us to ask how far, on Whewell's view, morality actually relies on intuition. At first the answer seems to be that it relies on it hardly at all. If someone asks why he ought to do some particular act, he will normally be referred (on Whewell's account) to a socially accepted rule, whether it be a rule of custom or one of law. If he challenges the rule, he will be referred to a more general rule of the same class, or he may be asked what grounds he has for objecting to the rule (since obedience to socially accepted rules is *prima facie* right). No intuition is invoked here: one may say that for the most part Whewell is not an

---

[82] *EMP*, 4th ed. (1864), Preface.
[83] *Ibid.*, para. 449.
[84] *Ibid.*, para. 450. Whewell also takes account of those who think of morality in terms of exemplary persons, and who hold that "good is what the good man does." See, e.g., *EMP*, para. 129; *Hist.*, p. 68.

act-intuitionist in the way that Mansel, for example, is. Is he then a rule-intuitionist? In one way he is not even that, because the content of the accepted rules of a society is largely the result, on his view, of historical circumstance and legal enactment. Still intuition does come into operation in connection with rules. Intuition enables us to tell whether a socially accepted rule conforms to the requirements of the basic axioms, the five aspects of the Supreme Rule. This might seem to be a matter for inference, not intuition, since the application of a criterion of adequacy to an instance is usually a matter of checking over the instance point by point, and weighing the result against the requirements. But the matter, according to Whewell, is more complicated when it comes to criticizing socially accepted rules as insufficiently just, or as not pure enough, or as not requiring a thorough enough honesty. The basic axioms, for Whewell, do not exist as yet in the form of fully articulated, clearly defined requirements. They are not yet what he calls "Express Principles," i.e., principles which we are prepared to state accurately. They are only (at best) "Operative Principles," i.e., principles which "operate in [a] man steadily and consistently, even though they be not expressed in words."[85] The criticism of an established rule *is* a mode of improving our express grasp of an operative fundamental axiom. If one asks for the basis or ground for criticism of an established rule, the only answer available is that one sees—dimly, no doubt—that it is not in conformity with the requirements of Justice, or Purity, or whatever, though perhaps no more than that can be said.

A similar point is brought out clearly and interestingly in Whewell's discussion of "hard cases" and what the moralist is to say about them. Allowing as we must that there occur cases in which established rules must be transgressed—where a lie must be told, a promise broken, a life taken—still, Whewell says, he will not attempt to define or enumerate such cases of necessity. For there are reasons why "the Moralist ought not to undertake such definition and enumeration." In cases like these there ought to be a struggle in the mind of the agent between the demands of morality and those of necessity. A virtuous man cannot "violate the broadest Rules of Morality, without pain and trouble of mind," and if he could, we would not find his transgression excusable. But if the moralist "were to define, beforehand, the conditions under which lying, or homicide, or submission to lust, is the proper course; those who accepted our Rules, would, when the occasion came, take that course without the reluctance and compunction, which are essential

[85] *EMP*, para. 161.

to make an act allowable in virtue of Necessity."[86] Cases of necessity would be transformed into ordinary rule-covered cases. But the disposition appropriate to such cases is wrong for cases of necessity. Hence the moralist ought not to make it possible to treat cases of necessity in that way. How then are decisions to be reached in hard cases? Whewell replies that "the course taken by the Actor will depend, and ought to depend, upon his state of Moral Culture."[87] For on this will depend the degree of his understanding of, or insight into, the fundamental axioms of morality. The difference between cases of necessity and cases in which criticism is directed against a socially accepted rule is not in the mode of reaching a decision, then, but rather in the extent to which the decision must be announced and clarified. In cases of social criticism, a consensus must be reached, or one's claim to have a better insight will hardly be justifiable. In cases of necessity, Whewell seems to think, the less said the better. The point is that in both kinds of case, where rules fail, there is nothing left but intuition to appeal to. There is no high order express principle in terms of which a discursive justification for making a change or an exception can be given.

Intuition is required, then, on Whewell's view, where there are questions of social criticism or cases of necessity. But more deeply it is required to explain the existence of morality at all, and to account for its progress. That the demand of morality is felt, even at the earliest stage, is due to the fact that men have some dim insight into the Idea of a Supreme Rule and some weak recognition of its authority. Man's moral progress, and our progress in understanding and systematizing it, both depend on the operation of this insight. Men are not infallible in this regard. It is for this reason that Whewell emphasizes so strongly the constant need for social consensus on moral belief. It is this which differentiates him, morally speaking, from an Intuitionist like Martineau who—strong-minded Dissenter that he is—has little use for social consensus, and which constitutes his greatest affinity with the Bradley of "My Station and Its Duties." But though it is not infallible, intuition is indispensible. Without it, on Whewell's view, men would not be capable of morality at all. And without possessing moral intuitions they could not follow the various steps which Whewell takes in the course of systematizing morality.[88]

---

[86] *Ibid.*, para. 317; cf. para. 322.
[87] *Ibid.*, para. 324.
[88] *LSM*, p. 106.

IX

Such, in outline, is Whewell's attempt at a systematization of the generally accepted morality. According to his own procedural views, we should now look for his *philosophy* of morality. If we do so, however, we are bound to be disappointed. Whatever the reason, he never constructed one. The actual application to morality of the general theory of knowledge developed in connection with the sciences, together with the brief remarks noted above concerning the differences between science and morality, constitute essentially the sum of Whewell's contribution to moral philosophy in its epistemological or "meta-ethical" aspect.

X

There are no doubt numerous criticisms to be made of Whewell's system of morality, aside from those concerned with awkwardness of style and ineptitude of presentation. To grant, as we must, that Mill and Martineau are unclear about Whewell's position and consequently quite mistaken in many of their criticisms, is not to give Whewell a clean bill of health. It is, however, not much to the point to criticize Whewell on points of detail. Whether his specific views on the basic desires and affections of mankind are sound or not, whether his interpretation of the relation of the imperatives of morality to the propositions of science is tenable, are questions which it would be profitless to discuss. Whether his method of constructing a system of morality by appealing to human nature, by seeing morality as a set of rules designed to regulate existing human desires with the aim of bringing humans to some ultimately desirable state of mind or soul, is acceptable, would not be profitless to discuss, but the discussion requires another context. There is, however, special point in an immediate attempt to assess Whewell's success or failure in doing what—if I am correct—he set out to do: to defend the "high" morality by showing how it could be allied with, instead of opposed to, the new science. The problem he here attempted to solve was the central problem of nineteenth century moral philosophy in England; and he was a sufficiently influential figure for his success or failure to have influenced the efforts of some of his successors.

A criticism made by Martineau will serve to start. Martineau objected to the proof that there must be moral rules—the proof which uses the premisses that man acts as man when he acts according to reason, and that reason is the faculty of rules—on the ground that its premisses are nothing but a "reprint of the definitions" and that the definitions are nothing but "an assumption of the point to be proved."[89] If this point has any value as a criticism it is in raising the question of the status of the concepts in terms of which Whewell systematizes common morality. Are these concepts theoretical constructs in a modern sense—useful devices, justified by their usefulness but claiming no other warrant? Or are they in some way more than that? There is at least no doubt what Whewell's answer to this question would be. He believes that the Ideas are metaphysically grounded. Our increasing grasp of the moral Ideas, as well as of the scientific ones, is not to be explained solely in terms of increase in ability to use a theory to explain more and more phenomena, or to make coherent more and more of morality. As the scientific Ideas are constitutive of the universe, so the moral Ideas are necessarily true in the same way as the laws of geometry and are constitutive of what ought to be. Our coming to know them is a coming to know in a full sense, not a construction. We may put this in another way by saying that God already knows all the Ideas fully and completely. The moral Ideas, at least, are not creations of God's will. To say that God is just and good is neither nonsense nor tautology: it is to say that God in some manner conforms to the Ideas of goodness and justice of which we too are aware, though dimly and darkly, and to which we strive also to conform. "We know what is the Will of God, by knowing what is right."[90] We are able to come to know the Ideas because our Reason is related to God's. Whewell says:

> The Reason, may be regarded as the image or participation of a Universal Reason . . . Reason . . . is not too highly spoken of, when we describe it as *An Image of the Divine mind*: for truths which we conceive as necessary and universal, we must conceive to be contemplated as truths by the Mind which framed the universe and created other minds.[91]

Whewell hastens to add that our reason is immeasurably imperfect compared with "the Divine Light." The imperfection affects the scientific reason and "still more is this true of that moral Reason which we ascribe to the soul of man."[92] Now although Whewell

---

[89] Martineau, *op. cit.*, pp. 369–370.
[90] *FM*, pp. 54–59; *LSM*, pp. 150–152.
[91] *Hist. Add.*, pp. 126–127.
[92] *Ibid.*, p. 130.

says that "the Moral Ideas exist in the Divine Mind in complete fullness and luminousness"[93] he gives no account of what is meant by this, nor of how moral ideas can thus exist. We cannot therefore hope to construct a complete reply to the questions posed by Martineau's criticism. We can however say this much. The definitions (of "man" and "reason") which Whewell relies on are presumably not purely arbitrary, nor are they merely reports of English usage: they are rather based on an insight, which Whewell assumes is shared, into the Ideas involved in our knowledge of man and reason. The same thing must hold of the crucial Idea of a Supreme Rule: Whewell's specification of it must not be arbitrary or reportive, but must be based on an insight into the Idea as it exists in God's mind, and his appeal to us to agree must rest on the proposition that all of us share in a common reason which in turn allows us to share his insight into this Idea.

If this is Whewell's view of the status of the Ideas, certain problems immediately arise for his system. Not the least, though perhaps the most obvious, is the question of the extent to which he has succeeded in showing that the "high" morality can be defended without reliance on outmoded metaphysical views. After all, if morality is made to depend on Ideas in the mind of God, how much advance has been made over Cumberland and Clarke? Whewell's reply to this would be, I take it, that he was attempting to show, not that morality can be supported independently of religion, but that morality is not in conflict with the findings and methods of modern science. Now science, he holds, depends on metaphysically grounded ideas too; and therefore, he thinks, the case is made out. This reply might force us to shift our criticism. We might be forced to attack the entire philosophy of science which Whewell proposes, in order to show that there is a split between morality and science. But we might take a different line, and raise the question whether, even granting Whewell's views on science, the parallel between science and morality can be made out. Whewell himself, after all, has pointed out that the kinds of truth in the two realms are quite different. Is he correct in assuming that despite this difference the two realms can be treated similarly in other respects?

He has himself pointed out one sort of difference between science and morality in their relation to progressive development. In science, he says, progress occurs because we try to fit our understanding of the Facts to the true Ideas which are relevant to them, in morality progress occurs as we succeed in making the Facts fit the demands

[93] *On the Philosophy of Discovery* (London, 1860), p. 387.

imposed by the moral Ideas. "Man's Intellectual Progress consists in the Idealization of Facts," Whewell says, "and his Moral Progress consists in the Realization of Ideas."[94] The implication of this is surely that we already know the moral Ideas, in a way in which we do not know the scientific Ideas. Now the plausibility of much of Whewell's systematization of morality comes from the claim that we do not fully know the moral Ideas, that moral progress through the use of positive law is necessary to our attainment of such knowledge, and that therefore disagreements which would otherwise tend to show that there is no intuitive power of apprehending moral truths can be explained by a general theory of a gradual approach to knowledge. Is this claim to be disallowed in general, or is it only to be disallowed for a privileged group who have reached final knowledge of the moral Ideas? Or are we to attribute Whewell's aphorism on the two kinds of progress to an unfortunate love of rhetorical balance? There are difficulties for either alternative.

(a) If we suppose that Whewell thinks we already have perfect knowledge of the moral Ideas, then the whole parallel with scientific knowledge seems to be struck down. We cannot discount disagreements about morality as we can those about geometry or physics, as due to lack of development. We cannot easily find criteria for selecting some special class of those who do have complete knowledge of the Ideas, so as to count only their opinions, and if we could, we could not use the idea of a developing consensus to bolster our appeal to intuition. The whole notion of the progressive moral education of mankind must take on a new light since some men, being already in possession of full moral knowledge, cannot need, but might disseminate, such education. Moreover, the whole historical aspect of the systematization of morality which Whewell gives is in principle unnecessary. It should have been given in a sort of introductory essay, and the bulk of the book should have been devoted to showing the true systematization in terms of the Ideas. I do not think that this procedure would have resulted in anything like Whewell's actual views.

(b) Whewell seems far more deeply attached to the other alternative, that there is still progress to be made in our understanding of the moral Ideas. He points out that the moral Ideas in the Divine Mind must be greatly elevated above those Ideas as they are in our minds; that we know of development already in our understanding of the moral Ideas, and may infer from the past that there is more

[94] *Ibid.*, p. 386.

progress to be made; and that we must suppose that both physical and moral Ideas as we have them only represent the divine Ideas "very incompletely and at an immeasurable distance." Our moral Ideas, he says, are "full of imperfections and inconsistency" which cannot be present in the divine mind.[95] This is, indeed, the theory underlying the whole reconstruction of morality in the *Elements*. And yet it poses problems. One is the problem of making intelligible, or perhaps acceptable, the notion that God's understanding of the moral Ideas may be different from ours. Whewell is acutely aware of this problem. When we say that God is just, we must take "just" to mean what we mean by it, Whewell says, and then, anticipating a famous passage of Mill, he says: "It would be absurd to combine the two propositions, that we necessarily believe that God is just, and that by *just* we mean something entirely different from the common meaning of the word."[96] But he gives no very clear account of how we are to reconcile this position with the belief that our group of the moral Ideas is radically defective. More immediately crucial is the problem of how, on this view, a report of interim progress toward an understanding of the moral Ideas can be a strong *defense* of a given morality. Is not our progress likely to be as surprising in morality as it is in science? Are we not likely to have revolutions as Copernican in the one area as in the other? Perhaps until now it has, in the light of actual facts, been plausible to say that though moral action will result in happiness, it cannot be derived from the principle of pursuing happiness. But tomorrow new facts could show that we must reverse our position. We might have to say that although moral action must be guided by rules even when the resulting acts do not in every case increase happiness, still the rules must ultimately be derived from and justified by the general principle of producing happiness.

The dilemma in short is this: if perfect moral knowledge already exists, then Whewell cannot defend moral intuitionism as he has tried to defend it (by relating it to a general intuitionism); and if perfect moral knowledge does not already exist, then he cannot help the "high" morality very much in its battle with utilitarianism. Unless we now have the final truth about morality, morality is as open to revolutionary change as science is. It is not without interest to note that Sidgwick, who knew Whewell's work well, devoted a major part of *The Methods of Ethics* to a searching examination of common sense

[95] *Ibid.*, pp. 387–393.
[96] *Ibid.*, p. 390.

morality, the upshot of which was that it could best be systematized by an appeal to *utilitarian* principles and that these principles could be seen to be intuitively acceptable.[97] Whether or not this was intended as in part a direct reply to Whewell, it is in any case a perfectly legitimate mode of turning his own method of argument against him.

University of Pittsburgh

---

[97] The examination of common sense morality in Book II of the *Methods of Ethics* was, Sidgwick says in the autobiographical fragment printed in the Preface to the Sixth Edition, the part of the book he wrote first.

Index of Names

Aristotle 39, 40, 65, 66, 88
Ayer, A. J. 10, 11, 12

Bacon, Francis 110
Baier, Kurt 12–24, 27, 30–33, 39, 41, 86
Baier, Mrs. Kurt 86
Bentham, Jeremy 66, 81, 108, 111, 118
Berger, Fred 26
Borelli, G. H. 112
Bradley, F. H. 135
Brandt, Richard 27, 39
Braybrooke, David 86–107
Braybrooke, W. L. 86
Broad, C. D. 26, 27, 30, 33, 109
Butler, Joseph 109, 111–12, 114, 121–2, 125
Butts, R. E. 109

Callicles 49
Chopra, Y. 56
Clarke, Samuel 110, 114, 138
Cooper, H. L. 51, 52
Cudworth, Ralph 114
Cumberland, Richard 112, 138

Descartes, René 110
Douglas, Mrs. S. 108
Ducasse, C. J. 109

Eliot, T. S. 40
Emerson, Ralph Waldo 86
Engels, Friederich 68, 86, 87

Forbes, D. 109
Frankena, William 27, 31, 53

Galbraith, J. K. 103, 104
Gewirth, Alan 68, 82
Grote, John 109, 132

Hare, R. M. 17, 18, 19, 39, 131
Hart, H. L. A. 68–70, 77
Haworth, Lawrence 64–85
Hegel, G. W. F. 131
Henderson, G. P. 42–51
Heracleitus 40
Herschel, J. F. W. 118
Hobbes, Thomas 68, 88, 110
Hume, David 67
Huyghens, Christian 112

Jarrell, Randall 86

Kalin, Jesse 26–41
Kant, Immanuel 17, 27, 35, 38, 39, 41, 68, 109, 126
Kepler, Johannes 112

Lindblom, C. E. 86
Locke, John 109, 110

Madden, E. H. 109
Mansel, Henry L. 134
Martineau, James 109, 113, 116, 117, 131, 135, 136
Marx, Karl 68
Maslow, A. H. 91
Medlin, Brian 27, 28–30

INDEX OF NAMES

Mill, John Stuart 54, 57, 68, 108–9, 111, 113, 117, 118, 128, 131, 136, 140
Minas, J. S. 64
Moore, G. E. 27, 109
Myers, F. 108

Nagel, Thomas 26
Narveson, J. F. 64
Newton, Isaac 110, 112
Nielsen, Kai 9–25

Paley, William 109
Pericles 104
Plantinga, Alvin 53
Plato 50, 52, 88
Popper, Karl 68

Rashdall, Hastings 56
Rawls, John 71–8
Rescher, Nicholas 7, 86
Ross, W. D. 39
Rousseau, J. J. 68
Russell, Bertrand 44

Sachs, D. 53

Schneewind, Jerome 86, 88, 108–41
Shakespeare, William 86
Sidgwick, Henry 27, 109, 112, 115, 132, 140–1
Skinner, B. F. 103
Sparshott, F. E. 86, 87, 88, 90, 91
Spencer, Herbert 68
Spinoza, Benedict 88
Stevenson, C. L. 10
Stocker, Michael 53–63

Taylor, Jeremy 110
Taylor, Paul 14, 15, 16, 18, 19, 23
Thrasymachus 49
Todhunter, Isaac 108, 119, 131
Tolman, E. C. 91
Tweedale, Martin 86

Urmson, J. O. 22, 53

West, Henry 53
Westermarck, E. A. 9, 10, 16, 19
Whewell, William 108–41

LIBRARY OF DAVIDSON COLLEGE

Books on regular loan may be checked out for **two weeks**. Books must be presented at the Circulation Desk in order to be renewed.

A fine of **five cents** a day is charged after date due.

Special books are subject to special regulations at the discretion of library staff.

OCT 3 0 1973							
JAN -5 1976							